"So many amazing ideas and moment... the way I think about sales leadership. It engages you from beginning to end, bridging the gap between framework and science."

—**ANDY KOFOID,** President, Global Field Operations at Databricks

"Now more than ever, organizations who prioritize customer success above all else will come out on top. *The Transparent Sales Leader* is a fantastic resource for those just beginning their sales careers, seasoned leaders, and everyone in between. This insightful book will transform your approach to leadership."

—**DJ PAONI,** President, SAP North America

"As if Todd couldn't get transparency in sales any clearer after his first book, he goes and writes a book on transparency in leadership, taking it to the next level! The breakdown of what it is and what it isn't, the 'Five F's Framework,' and the cherry on top of what leadership that matters truly looks like in practice made it difficult for me to put the book down. Whether you're thinking about getting into leadership or have been in the game for years, this is a must-read book where you'll get better as a result."

—**AMY VOLAS,** Founder & CEO, Avenue Talent Partners and Co-Founder of Thursday Night Sales

"Certain words are used in business so thoughtlessly that they have become devoid of meaning: Authentic. Real. Transparent. And there is no one I trust more to rescue them than Todd Caponi. In this most recent book, he erects upon the foundation he poured in *The Transparency Sale* a sales leadership framework of such astounding utility and obvious value as to be almost self-evident. I buy a copy of his book for sellers for every rep I hire or mentor, and I will buy this book for every sales leader I work with. Todd's work is as compelling and useful as any business book I have ever read."

—**ETHAN ZOUBEK,** Chief Revenue Officer, Atari

"*The Transparent Sales Leader* is a modern playbook for maximizing the revenue potential of your teams. If you hate complex, hard-to-implement leadership books with lots of theory and little how-to—you're going to love this book."

—JASON BAY, Founder, Outbound Squad

"*The Transparent Sales Leader* provides straightforward advice, examples, and best practices for any modern sales leader, new or experienced. This is a refreshing guide for how to build trust and high-performing organizations in today's landscape."

—JEFF ROSSET, Founder & CEO, Sales Assembly

"*The Transparency Sale* quickly became required reading for sales professionals everywhere. With *The Transparent Sales Leader*, Todd Caponi has miraculously caused lightning to strike twice. Often counterintuitive but backed up by compelling research and actionable takeaways, Todd provides sales leaders a step-by-step guide on how to build and lead high-performing teams while making the job of a sales leader—one of the most stressful and underappreciated roles in any industry—much more enjoyable to execute."

—MATT GREEN, Chief Revenue Officer, Sales Assembly

"It's an exciting time for women in sales as we are beginning to get more and more curious about sales—and sales leadership! As you continue to explore the career—and leadership opportunities—Todd's easy-to-follow leadership framework is a must! It will optimize your career and give you that competitive edge!"

—TANIA DOUB, Founder & CEO, Work It! and Author of *Work It, Girl!*

"Todd Caponi is one of the most affable, down-to-earth people you'll ever meet. In *The Transparent Sales Leader*, he'll punch you right between the eyes with the truth about effective sales leadership, back it all up with science and a smile, and you'll thank him for it."

—JEFF BAJOREK, Consultant, Author, Podcast Host, *Rethink The Way You Sell*

"Todd Caponi has always been a top performer in the sales leadership field. In our work together over 15 years, I've watched how his 'done right' sales leadership has massively impacted his career, his companies, and those he has served. This book shows you how, in an insightful, engaging framework and science-forward way. A must-read for any revenue leader who's serious about their craft."

—SCOTT ANSCHUETZ, CEO & Founder, Visualize, Inc. for ValueSelling

HOW THE POWER OF SINCERITY, SCIENCE, AND STRUCTURE CAN TRANSFORM YOUR SALES TEAM'S RESULTS

IDEAPRESS
PUBLISHING

Published in the United States by Ideapress Publishing.

Ideapress Publishing | www.ideapresspublishing.com

Cover Design: Paul Nielsen, Faceout Studio

Cataloging-in-Publication Data is on file with the Library of Congress.

ISBN: 978-1-64687-111-7 (Paperback)
ISBN: 978-1-64687-064-6 (Hardcover)

Special Sales
Ideapress Books are available at a special discount for bulk purchases for sales promotions and premiums, or for use in corporate training programs. Special editions, including personalized covers, a custom foreword, corporate imprints, and bonus content, are also available.

1 2 3 4 5 6 7 8 9 10

The Transparent Sales Leader

TODD CAPONI

IDEAPRESS
PUBLISHING

WASHINGTON, D.C.

CONTENTS

To my dad,

the original transparent sales leader

INTRODUCTION

It is worse than futile—it is foolish for you to imitate anybody else. Just be your best self. Make the most of what you have that is salable. You require no more to assure your success.

— Norval A. Hawkins, *Certain Success*, 1910

"We think you're ready."

It was the middle of the night in Germany, where I was conducting training for one of our partners. My co-worker, Mark, was banging on my hotel room door to wake me up. My phone's SIM card wasn't functioning, so attempts from my CEO to reach me were going unanswered.

"Todd, Michael is on the phone. He needs to speak with you right now!"

The company was struggling, consistently underperforming the great expectations set by our Silicon Valley investors. Michael informed me of the departure of our senior vice president of sales. He was handing the reins of the sales organization over to me. The responsibility for driving the revenue that would keep the entire organization afloat and the investors financially above water was now mine.

I was not selected because I was a consistent top sales performer. It was not because of my age and experience, either. I was in my 30s, which made me younger than every single person I would now be overseeing. It also had nothing to do with the extensive training I had received in sales leadership. I had never received any.

Sales leadership was always my goal. Two years earlier, during my second day on the job, I had shared this desire with Michael during a random interaction. During a drive together, I explained to him how I had a deep background in sales, sales training, and learning science. However, I knew I had never been trained in sales leadership, nor did I possess any experience running a real team. Part of my decision to join this organization was to learn under the SVP of sales, see how it's done, and eventually work my way into a similar role. Michael remembered.

Reality set in the following day. My lack of training, and most importantly, two gaping holes awaited me in my attempts to be the best sales leader I could be.

The first? I always had a sales process and structure to fall back on. However, now what process or structure would I be following? I was aware of the immediate challenges to be addressed. We had to grow the team, establish and meet a forecast, prepare for a board meeting, and look into how we are executing our mission. What about the piles of unknown challenges I wouldn't even know to see?

The second? My personality was tuned for sales. Did I need a different personality to drive the performance of a team? I was no longer a peer to the team. How would I make the transition, drive performance, and minimize turnover?

As you have graduated to the role of sales leadership, there is a quick realization that the two roles of sales and sales leadership could not be more opposite:

Sales is the ultimate *independent* role. You are your organization's voice to the prospective buyer. You are the Sherpa to the prospective buyer's journey. You define your own success. You are transferring confidence to the buyer.

Sales leadership is the ultimate *dependent* role. Your success is dependent on the success of those you lead. You are transferring confidence to your sellers.

Revenue leaders have traditionally fallen back on what they've learned from their past leaders. So, the telephone game of sales leadership skills happens, eroding with each generation.

So I created a structure. Over the years of its use, I added in behavioral science, research, and data to modify and support the system. Magic happened. I began to see holes before they formed. Instead of chasing, I was growing. And so was the team. Turnover amongst the sales team fell to near zero. Everyone around me started using the structure, up to and including my CEO. In my executive sales leadership roles, transparent communications were born from the framework. Even our board would come to expect it as the guide for our agenda, which built their confidence in our sales execution strategy. Later, when I interviewed against 13 other chief revenue officer candidates for my last role, I was the only one who came in with a framework, a plan. According to the existing leadership team and the board, I was an A+ candidate, and nobody else was even a C grade. I'm not convinced I was any better than the other candidates, but having a framework sure helped!

To maximize sales team and organizational performance, we need to optimize five core areas required to build, maximize, and maintain revenue capacity. Sales leadership does not have to be that hard. There is a set of core responsibilities, which we will explore, that can quickly become your structure when categorized. There are also a core set of drivers to intrinsic inspiration—the science of why your team continues to show up each day, perform at their best, stay, and advocate.

The Transparent Sales Leader challenges long-held sales leadership standards, providing a modern, cards-faceup, science-backed, easy-to-implement framework for today's sales leaders. It will become your means of planning, strategizing, and communicating. You'll see the holes before they form. You will sound really smart, too!

You will also learn the science behind intrinsic inspiration. Becoming a transparent sales leader relies on a commitment to transparency, humbleness, and sincerity. I wasn't going to be anyone's boss. We were all equals. We just have different responsibilities.

It will become your sales leadership process if you let it. We'll work through each step in the process, with resources within each which I hope you can continue to refer to as a handbook for your career. Embrace it. Make it your own. And when you do, you will set yourself apart in pursuing sales leadership opportunities. In the role, you will always have an instant 30-60-90-day plan. If you're a leader-of-leaders, you will have a framework to structure onboarding for new managers, categorize your business plan for your board, senior leadership team, and the entire organization. You can structure every one-on-one with your other leaders or your bosses. You will gain ideas for structuring organizations, avoiding "science projects," and get better results from forecasting.

I wrote this book to be the foundation for new sales managers, challenge the long-held standards associated with the leadership position, be a reference guide of ideas and refreshers for seasoned managers, and a vessel to maximize the sales capacity of entire organizations for sales leadership.

The Transparent Sales Leader offers a framework centered around those five areas for your first-to-fiftieth sales leadership roles. Transparent sales leadership is for those who believe that hitting revenue targets isn't the job, it's the outcome. I break the book into three primary sections.

PART 1: THE TRANSPARENT SALES LEADER FRAMEWORK

In Part 1, we learn and develop the filing system in your brain for the five categories of responsibilities in sales leadership for which all things reside: the "Five F's of Maximizing Revenue Capacity." Once internalized, you will immediately be equipped to better plan, strategize, and communicate in all directions; your one-on-ones, your board meetings (when you get there, if not already), your interviews, your due diligence projects, and so much more. You will see the holes before they form.

Within each of the Five F's, I will equip you with the tools to maximize each responsibility. If all you did was read and internalize Part 1, you will immediately be 98% ahead of every other sales leader who wakes up each morning chasing solutions to the fires of the day.

Although, you may want to stick around for Part 2 . . .

PART 2: THE BEHAVIORAL SCIENCE OF INTRINSIC INSPIRATION

As a sales and revenue leader, the minute you truly understand how your team members are driven beyond the dollars, they'll stay longer, perform better, and more likely advocate for the role to their friends . . . which speeds time to hire, too. Just like how I took the responsibilities of a sales leader and categorized them into a structure for the role, I did the same thing with the drivers that establish, maintain, and maximize intrinsic inspiration. We'll go through each of the elements that drive our teams and us to maximize performance, tenures, your culture, and advocacy of yourself and your team. Let's learn them, along with ways to apply each to your selling environment.

PART 3: MYTHS AND APPLICATIONS

In the third part of the book, we bust the myths of sales motivation, then explore ways to take these learnings to extend your lead. This will help you get and keep the next big opportunity in your career—from interviewing to motivating your team to managing the board.

PART ONE

THE TRANSPARENT SALES LEADER FRAMEWORK

CHAPTER 1

TRANSPARENCY DEFINED

Be human. The reason you are hired to sell goods is that you are a human being. Otherwise your employer would have sent a catalogue.

— Dr. Frank Crane, *The Ten Commandments of Salesmanship*, 1918

A S HUMAN BEINGS, WE ARE PREDICTION MACHINES. FROM THE TIME WE are babies, our brains are wired to predict. We use those predictions to learn and as the basis for our satisfaction. Our hearts beat faster in anticipation of moving from a seated position to standing up. We learn by configuring a prediction, observing reality, comparing our prediction to that reality, then consolidating those learnings for storage for the next time.

When our brains struggle to predict, we want to seek solid, sure ground.

Flashback to March of 2020, when it became clear that lockdowns from Covid-19 were imminent, millions rushed to the store to hoard toilet paper. Solid ground, in that case, consisted of a pantry filled with the comfort of two-ply.

Satisfaction comes from consistency and predictability. When we can predict, our brain is optimized for doing what we must do.

In a work environment, our IQ is at its highest in environments where we can predict.[1] We perform better and are more likely to stay and advocate.

Could the secret of revenue leadership success begin with something as simple as accurate expectation setting? It's a great place to start. The brains of the individuals you lead are optimized when they can make a confident prediction as to what their experience in that moment and in the future is going to be.

A prediction is hard to come by when the recipient is having trouble trusting the source. The more the individual reporting to you can trust you as the source, the more discretionary effort the individual will put in—not only to help themselves, but also to help you.

TRANSPARENT LEADERSHIP LESSONS FROM ECOMMERCE, AND SUPERMODELS?

If you have read *The Transparency Sale*, you likely know all about the overused word, *transparency*. My passion for this concept began in my last role as chief revenue officer of Chicago's PowerReviews, Inc. PowerReviews is the engine behind the collection and display of ratings and reviews on over 1,000 retailers' and brands' websites.

In 2016, we engaged with Northwestern University to investigate how consumers interact with a website when that website is acting as the salesperson. In other words, when we as consumers shop online, and our interaction is only with the website itself, what do we do? Three core data points resulted from this study,[2] two of which changed my life in a way that could only happen to a nerd like me. This study was the spark that caused me to quit my job to write my first book.

When a website is acting as a salesperson:

Data point 1: Almost all (96%) of consumers read reviews before purchasing a service or product they haven't bought before. In other words, we all read reviews! I was not surprised by the first data point, other than that 4% of consumers did not read reviews. However, in PowerReviews' 2021 update to this study, this percentage was at 99.9%.[3]

Data point 2: As many as 82% of consumers seek out negative reviews. When a website acts as the salesperson, we as consumers and potential buyers choose to skip past the 5-star feedback and instead read the 4's, 3's, 2's and 1's. In the latest update to this research, this number is now up to 96%.

Data point 3: The optimal average star rating for purchase probability is between 4.2–4.5 on a 5-star scale. In other words, a product with negative reviews listed right alongside the product itself aids the consumer in triggering a purchase decision. A product with an average review score of 4.2 will sell at a higher conversion rate than a product with nothing but glowing, 5-star reviews. A recent addition to this research concluded that 46% of shoppers are consciously suspicious of products with an average star rating of five out of five.[4]

Again, that was when a website was acting as a salesperson. So, I went on a journey to find out why, with a specific question in mind: If transparency and imperfection help a product sell better when a website is acting as a salesperson, would the same be true when a human being is driving a decision in an individual, whether it be in a sales capacity, or any situation where one person is trying to influence another?

The answer was emphatically *yes*. In every interaction, we are either building trust or eroding it. Our instinct is to maintain the status quo because it is certain. As a result, we use logic or data to support our prevailing opinion. It's a shortcut the brain desires, given that the brain comprises just 2% of our body's weight,[5] but uses 20% of its energy sources (the oxygen and blood).

At even a subconscious level, we know that perfection isn't probable. When assessing an investment in our time, resources, or dollars in something new, our brain goes on a journey to decide, "Is the juice going to be worth the squeeze?" However, our brain filters the good news until it has assessed the trade-off, which could be the price, what elements or features are not included, and what experiences others have had—especially the negative.

The negatives act as a disarming mechanism. It is almost as though a malarkey filter has been removed, where the positives and benefits of this decision can now flow freely.

In 1995, a company you may have heard of, Amazon, was the first to embrace listing the negative feedback right alongside the products they were selling (along with the positive feedback, of course).[6] They've seemingly done well.

It works online. It works in human-to-human selling. It works in leadership.

And, due to the pervasiveness of reviews, feedback, networking, and human connection, we can no longer hide the flaws, downsides, unfortunate events, and experiences and expect to get away with it, anyway.

Transparency sells better than perfection, retains better, upsells and cross-sells better, creates advocates better, and leads better.

Transparency is not about beginning every conversation by proclaiming to the world, "Hey, this is why we/I suck!" Take it easy. Who wants to run behind someone who sucks? And even worse, who wants to run behind someone with so little self-confidence?

It starts with the wisdom of a supermodel. Yes, here we will impart a term most typically attributed to Tyra Banks. Banks, a television personality, model, business mogul, producer, and actress, often uses the word "flawsome": "An individual who embraces their 'flaws' and knows they are awesome regardless."

The 4.2–4.5 star-rating range discussed above is an important distinction. While that rating is an average across all product categories and skews higher or lower based on the product being sold, it still feels pretty good, right?

As a sales leader, transparency starts with an understanding that you are flawsome. You are worth running behind. However, you are human, too.

In one study, the relationship between leadership "transparency" and "employee happiness" had a .937 correlation coefficient.[7] What does that mean, in less nerdy terms? The term "correlation coefficient" is used to calculate how strong the relationship is between two data points. The score is always between -1 and 1.

- -1 means there's a negative relationship between the two. Being "randomly tased at work" would likely have a -1 correlation coefficient with "employee happiness."
- 0 would mean there is no relationship at all.
- However, a 1 would mean a complete overlap in relationship.

Transparent leadership, when done correctly, has the most significant correlation to building, maintaining, and growing a team. So, at .937, transparency is almost *equal* to employee happiness. And, without transparency, engagement and enjoyment at work suffers mightily.

Traditionally, sales organizations have kept their team members on a need-to-know basis. A salesperson is delivered a job description, a territory, some training, metrics to hit, the tools and resources to do it, and becomes an "employee ID number" with a "sales target number." However, sales leaders monumentally underestimate their sales team members' ability to see through a muddling of the facts. It may be one of the top skills of a great salesperson. The result is disengagement and likely turnover.

Transparent leadership is living the following values every single moment, consistently:

- Taking a cards-faceup approach to leadership.
- Setting proper expectations, consistently meeting them, and embracing the idea that those expectations are not always just rainbows and cotton candy.
- Embracing the idea that you do not have all the answers.
- Embracing the idea that you have weaknesses, and it's ok for others to know that.
- Embracing the idea that you are no more important than anyone else on the team, you just have different responsibilities.

In your role as a sales leader, you are both a leader and being led. You still report to someone, right? Even if you're the CEO, you likely report to a board, investors, or potentially a chairperson. As an entrepreneur, I report to my wife and children. I have given myself a quota each quarter as a measuring stick, but not hitting my quarterly quota has far-reaching ramifications at home.

Imagine your leader sharing her approach to leadership with you. Imagine her explaining how she approaches the job each day, what she uses to measure and predict the future proactively, how to strategize, see opportunities, and assess weaknesses and threats. Would that make you more comfortable, or less?

Imagine your leader sharing where she believes her strengths are, and where she falls short. Imagine her explaining what she is doing to up-skill and asking for your help in her personal and professional development. Imagine your leader embracing their "flawsome" with you and your peers. Would that make you more comfortable, or less? Would these qualities drive you intrinsically to stay, perform your best each day, and advocate for what you do?

According to behavioral science, research, data, and practical application, the answer is likely *yes*!

It's not difficult for you to become the transparent sales leader. There is almost zero cost to being transparent as a leader. In the end, the more transparency you give, the more you'll get in terms of reciprocal transparency, engagement, performance, tenure, and advocacy.

TRANSPARENCY—WHAT IT ISN'T

A considerable portion of our responsibility as sales leaders centers around expectation setting: helping our team predict their day, week, month, and even future; helping our managers and leaders predict; helping our board predict; helping our investors predict.

Overpromising and underdelivering is, of course, an unsustainable policy. When the local meteorologist tells me it is going to be 75°F and sunny over the weekend,

I plan accordingly. When I wake up Saturday morning to 32°F and snow, my satisfaction for that individual, trust in what they tell me, and the costs associated with those mis-set expectations is profound.

However, consistently underpromising and overdelivering is also unsustainable. It will typically produce a short-term spike in satisfaction, but it leads to something I like to call "expectation inflation." Technically, it is a form of lying.

Expectation inflation is when we consistently underpromise and overdeliver. As recipients of the expectation being set, we will subconsciously expect more than the expectation.

My wife and kids went to a new restaurant that opened around 15 minutes from our home. The expectation for any restaurant during a first visit is prompt service, friendly interactions, a nice atmosphere, good food, then, we receive the check and go home. This restaurant checked all those boxes. However, there was a surprise at the end. Along with the check came freshly baked chocolate chip cookies and milk for the kids. The expectation was the check. The reality was something far better. The kids were wowed. The cookies were soft, warm, with just the right volume of chocolate chips. They were now sold. We are coming back.

The next time we went to this restaurant, the check came with the cookies once again. The kids were less excited because those cookies constituted the new expectation. Anything less would be a disappointment. Sure enough, during our third visit, the cookies came with the check, but they weren't fresh this time. Clearly, these cookies didn't just come out of the oven. They tasted great to my wife and I, but the kids were disappointed. No other restaurant we visit provides anything other than a mint with the check. However, my children were upset with the quality of the cookie. Is that a failure in parenting? No. It's ultimately the challenge of sustaining the underpromise/overdeliver.

Why? Because exceeding expectations becomes the new expectation.

Prior to my first sales leadership role, I joined a sales organization on the same day as their quarterly sales kickoff. Each rep was required to get up and give their "commit" on day two. We will discuss later in the book why this dated practice does much more harm than good for your team's engagement, motivation, and especially your forecast and longer-term performance. However, as each rep spoke up during this meeting, you could see the dynamic of expectation setting in action at a human level.

Jessie, who consistently crushed her quarterly number, was one of the first to present. It was clear that she was hiding deals. Her quarterly target was $300,000. She committed to $320,000. In looking in the CRM, her pipeline progress indicated that she would do considerably better than $320,000. At the team dinner that evening, I asked her about it. I was curious about the mismatch between what I saw in the CRM and her estimate for the commit. She responded, "I don't want everyone's eyes on me and my deals all quarter, so I underpromise, then overdeliver."

Our sales leader shared the consolidated commits from all the team members with me the next day. I scrolled down to Jessie's name, and sure enough, he wrote $420,000. So I said, "I had $320,000 written down for Jessie."

He replied, "I know Jessie."

At the end of the quarter, Jessie finished at around $400,000. She hit her quarterly target. She exceeded her commit. However, she disappointed the leader because she did not hit the expectation-inflation amount he predicted. Consistently underpromising and overdelivering sets a new expectation, one that is wholly unsustainable.

There is magic in setting expectations and consistently meeting them.

THE AUTHENTIC LEADER MYTH

There's a big difference between "authentic" leadership and "transparent" leadership. Let's start with authenticity first.

This chapter started with a quote from Dr. Frank Crane: "Be human. The reason you are hired to sell goods is that you are a human being. Otherwise your employer would have sent a catalogue."

Being authentic is to "be true to the self." Authenticity is about bringing your true self to every interaction and decision. It's about being consistent with your own beliefs and personal values. It's about being frank and honest, allowing people to see the true you. That's a good thing in life and sales.

However, as a sales leader, it can be the downfall of your effectiveness for your team and your company. Becoming an authentic leader heightens the risk of becoming preoccupied with yourself versus focusing on the needs and wants of others.

In other words, an authentic leader runs the risk of bringing their values and beliefs, including moral stances, to stand for the vision and mission of the team instead of the organizational values. An authentic leader runs the risk of prioritizing their own thinking. An authentic leader soon falls into the trap of caring about their team only to the point where they help themselves achieve their own goals. The authentic leader runs the risk of becoming "too authentic."[8] Those who have a narcissistic streak can abuse the virtues of authenticity.

If authenticity is bringing your true self to every interaction, as a friend of mine once asked, "What if your true self is an imbecile?" What if you are lacking in experience, respectfulness, and tact? What if your team doesn't yet respect you? What if you're an authentic incompetent?

Don't buy into the hype that authenticity in leadership is the solution to future aspirational leadership. Yes, you should always be yourself. However, prioritize transparency over authenticity.

THE ROLE

Your entire being is designed with safety as the one priority. Think about it. The reptilian brain, housed in the center of your head, has safety mechanisms that trigger before you can ever even think about them consciously. You're reading this book, and a snake slithers into the room. Your body will react before you realize it. Touch a hot stove. Your hand will retract considerably faster than you realize the pain. The human brain's priority is safety over success. However, when describing success, the word *safe* doesn't often get listed among the traits of said success.

You are a sales leader. Your number one job is to move people toward successful outcomes—professionally and personally. That begins with trust. You won't run behind anyone you don't trust. However, much of that movement you are responsible for is housed in a need to push those individuals into decisions that may be a subconscious threat to their own perceived safety. There's an anxiety in making a cold call, potentially a stage-fright threat of doing a presentation or demonstration to an audience of potential buyers, a discomfort of talking about and negotiating pricing or contract terms. There could even be anxiety around trying new things, stretching yourself to take on a new responsibility or the pressure of a questionable goal.

Your team must trust that you can get them to those successful outcomes before they will take the subconscious risks required to get them there. Trust begins with transparency through the setting of accurate expectations. Help team members embrace the anxiety.

At my local gym, I overheard one of the personal trainers working with a new client. She built trust in her customer's journey to their successful outcome by predicting the pain.

"I'm going to have you do some things today to failure."

"You'll probably wake up sore tomorrow morning, and the next day may be even worse. However, through consistency, not only will the soreness stop, but you'll also probably replace it with some pretty cool endorphins instead."

In sales leadership, trust is built through expectation setting, embracing both the good and the bad. "Here's what might hurt on your way to your goal." "The outbound calls are probably going to suck at first until you get the hang of it." "Deals will be lost and goals may not be met. That's ok! We're going to learn from each, and make sure we use each to help us achieve our goal."

Transparent leadership requires a cards-faceup approach to the role, the company, the challenges, and you, personally—both to your team, but also to those above you.

Think about it. When you start your first sales leadership role, you will acquire more power. The power swings become more dramatic with those responsibilities. As you have more power with your team and their outcomes, but feel a more dramatic swing when you meet with your manager, their manager, and maybe even a board. Transparency down . . . and up, helps to alleviate the swings.

Every individual and every situation is a tradeoff. There is always something given up in exchange for all that goodness. Acknowledging and sharing is where trust begins. Remember, a product with negative reviews right alongside the product sells better than a product presented as perfection. The same holds true for you as a leader.

TRANSPARENCY BEGETS TRANSPARENCY

Two years ago, I bought a new car. Well, it wasn't quite new . . . it was a never-owned 2018 Ford Explorer. I found this car on the dealer's website. It was the model I wanted, the color I wanted, and in the price range that I wanted. The good news for me was it wasn't the only car that fit my criteria amongst the vicinity of Ford dealers within 25 miles of my home. In other words, I wasn't wed to this specific car. And, as a transparency nerd, I was dying to try to embrace transparency as a buyer. Having a theory about what might happen, I brought a notebook with me to take notes.

Upon entering the showroom, I was assigned a salesperson. We'll call him Frankie (because that was his name). Frankie was a younger guy, sharp, knew the cars up-and-down, articulate, but could stand to take it easy on the cologne.

With a simple Google search, you'll find articles outlining the three things often said about purchasing a car that a buyer should never do:

1. Never share how you plan to pay for the vehicle until *after* you have agreed to the price.
2. Never share your intention to trade-in a used vehicle until *after* you have agreed to the price.
3. And, for goodness' sake, *never* share the details of what's wrong with your trade-in vehicle. Let the dealer find those issues on their own—with

fingers-crossed that they won't find the problem and offer you more than the car is worth.

Knowing I had seven different vehicles that matched my desires, also knowing what I was willing to pay for each, I decided to throw those three rules out the window.

Upon sitting down with Frankie, I immediately broke rule 1 by informing him of my intention to pay cash (i.e., write a check) for the purchase. I had the dollars all worked out. I was ready to buy.

I also immediately informed Frank of my intention to trade in my 2011 Jeep Grand Cherokee Laredo. I pointed to it in the parking lot, breaking rule 2. And in the same sentence, I also broke rule 3.

"Frankie, see that smoke still swirling in your parking lot and behind my car? That's from my Jeep."

Quite literally, my car barely made it to the dealership that day. I didn't even know a car had this capability, but instead of the "check engine" light simply turning on, it was flashing. I later learned that this happens when the situation is dire.

Breaking all three rules in the first three minutes of the discussion, what happened next was remarkable. Frankie, within the next 15 minutes, became instantly more transparent with me. He shared with me his issues with ADHD (attention deficit hyperactivity disorder), which can lead to limited attention and hyperactivity. He then shared with me issues in his relationship with his father, then concerns about his job and his career. Taking advantage of the situation, as we got just a little deeper into a discussion about the car itself, I asked him about his compensation plan. Without hesitation, he shared it with me.

Transparency begets transparency. Transparency builds trust, leading to faster sales and clients who stay, buy more, and advocate for you. Transparency also drives employees to bring their best selves to work every day, stay, and advocate for what they do. But those results don't occur unless transparency starts with every leader in the organization. At the team level, when you embrace transparency, you'll find your team is more transparent with your customers and prospects and with you. The result is a better relationship, a better environment, better results, faster time to hire, and even a more accurate forecast!

We, as consumers, don't trust the five-star reviews when a website is acting as the salesperson. We seek the negative reviews first, which builds trust, creates expectations, and allows the positive aspects of a potential purchase to better resonate with the consumer. The same is true in human-to-human sales. And even more importantly, the same is true in human interactions.

Reveal to your team your specific responsibilities as a leader, your strategy, your plan, and the way you think about the role. Build trust through transparency, then use that same transparency to set proper expectations. You are the light in a dark forest. Your team becomes the moths.

With transparency firmly defined, let's now learn the framework we'll use to structure, strategize, and communicate.

CHAPTER 2

THE FIVE F'S FRAMEWORK

*I believe I would be well within the bounds of conservatism if
I told them that one million dollars per day was being wasted
through the wrong sort of sales method.*

— C. W. Hoyt, *Scientific Sales Management*, 1918

T'S YOUR FIRST DAY IN YOUR NEW SALES LEADERSHIP ROLE. YOU ARE assigned a quarterly revenue target to achieve. "Here is your team. Here is the territory your team is responsible for covering. Go."

Go. It is as though a car had just passed by your house, and you are a dog chasing it down the street. It turns left, and so do you. It stops for a stop sign, so you almost catch up, but then it turns again, and off you go.

As you begin to dig in, the priorities pile up. Jini doesn't seem to be getting it. Jessica appears to be an all-star but doesn't keep the CRM system up to date, so you have no idea what's happening. Jackie doesn't seem to like or respect you, and you're unsure why; she's just not listening. Jasper just started two weeks ago, so you better spend some time making sure he's acclimating well. Your days look like your high school class schedule. Meeting. Clock strikes the top of the hour. Head to your next meeting.

You think, "My last meeting of the day today is with my new manager. She's gonna need to know the sales forecast." Do you want to impress her with your knowledge of the team, the accounts, and their status already? Or do you want to buy yourself some time? You never catch up—until you change jobs. Then it starts over.

Your levels of stress go up. Your confidence goes down. Stress is contagious, and so is confidence.

When you are experiencing a state of feeling like stress, joy, fear, or confidence, similar to germs, others around you can sense it both consciously and subconsciously. When we, as human beings, sense the state of another person, that state also lights up in our own brains.[9] As a result, we feel what the individual we're interacting with feels. In other words, the individuals who are sensing your stress experience stress as a result.

Transferring confidence to your sellers is a key function of your role. Ideally, to be an optimally effective sales leader, understanding this effect is, well, everything! As a sales leader, you are responsible for transferring confidence to your team. The salespeople on your team are responsible for transferring confidence to their potential clients.

But you must have the right amount of confidence. A lack of confidence becomes a germ that travels through your team and onto your prospects and clients. However, have you ever been around someone with too much confidence? That may be even worse!

To start, the word *confidence* has two primary definitions:

1. "A feeling of self-assurance arising from one's appreciation of one's own abilities or qualities"[10]
2. "The feeling or belief that one can rely on someone or something; firm trust"[11]

Both definitions firmly define confidence as a feeling. But what's so interesting about the difference between the two is, in the first definition, confidence is something you possess *within yourself*. In the second definition, confidence is something that is recognized by others, finishing with the words, "firm trust."

Your sellers are configuring their expectations of success through you and through their teammates. Your prospects and customers are configuring their expectations of success through those sellers.

INSTILLING CONFIDENCE

Unfortunately, you can't learn how to *appear* confident. You can't fake it (although scientists are working on it[12]). Perhaps you've seen the highly watched TED Talk from 2012[13] claiming that you can practice body language and "power poses" to improve perceptions of self-confidence (as of this writing, it's been watched over 61 million times); that has been debunked as well.[14]

Confidence begins with the words from the first definition above—an "appreciation of one's own abilities." Knowing your job, with a predictable structure, a plan, and a way to communicate it will set you far apart from others with similar responsibilities. You'll have confidence. That structure, created and used in a transparent way, will create the confidence your sellers so need through "the feeling or belief that one can rely on someone or something."

What is that structure? Well, I'm glad you asked. It's the Five F's of Maximizing Revenue Capacity.

THE FIVE F'S: FOCUS, FIELD, FUNDAMENTALS, FORECAST, FUN

This, the Five F's, is the scope of your role. Every responsibility you have fits into it. It is your ultimate responsibility, and it is never perfect. But with a structure, you are no longer the dog chasing the car; you are the car with the map.

From this structure, you can ensure you've got your bases covered coupled with a way to always be at the ready to articulate it.

You will make sure your team is working on the right opportunities at the right time through your efforts to hone the team's *focus*. You'll lead the *field* each day with the right people in the right roles in the right places with the right tools and the right resources through your efforts to build it. Your team will consistently execute through your efforts to drive the *fundamentals*. You will predict the future through measuring the right KPIs and metrics engrossing your responsibility to *forecast*. And you will drive *fun* through the creation, management, and optimization of an environment where your team is intrinsically inspired, so they'll show up, do their best, stay, and tell their friends.

Everything you do as a sales leader falls into one of those five categories. As you begin your new role, take inventory of each. Prioritize them. Next, we'll dig into each at a summary level, then give you tips, tools, and new ways to think about each category in the chapters ahead.

However, if you choose to nod off to sleep right now, do a first pass at simply memorizing the five: focus, field, fundamentals, forecast, and fun. As we'll discuss more throughout the rest of this book, even if you never read another word, you're now ahead of 98% of your peers. Let's extend your lead . . .

1) FOCUS

Ensure the team has focus, spending their time on the right opportunities in the right places at the right time. The individuals you will lead have an inventory of time. It is the most valuable asset they own. How is that inventory being allocated? You are responsible for establishing, maintaining, and optimizing your team's effort so none of it is wasted.

When the team wakes up in the morning, how do they prioritize who they will go after that day? What industries? What geographies? What sizes? What individuals within those organizations? How do they know those are the right priorities? As leads come in, how do the reps know which ones are worth investing their time on, and which are not?

2) FIELD

Structure your field organization to maximize effectiveness, efficiency, and output. Ensuring you are deploying the right team with the right tools and the right resources to best address your focus. You cannot determine whether you have the right team until you've established the basis for having the right focus.

The investment in talent, tools, and surrounding support is quite possibly the most expensive investment in your entire organization. Is it optimized for the ideal focus?

3) FUNDAMENTALS

It's on you to ensure the field organization you've invested so much into is doing the fundamentals right. Maximum output requires the right execution, done consistently. Start with the foundational elements. If you were at a party, and one of your team members was asked, "Hey, what does your company do?", would the answer scare you? How good is your team at uncovering new opportunities (prospecting)? Think about their presenting skills, qualification skills, negotiation, and overall sales process execution. It's on you to coach your team to get the right things right, consistently.

Now, finally, it's time to figure out the numbers . . . or in other words, the . . .

4) FORECAST

Quite possibly the most obvious of your assumed responsibilities, you must be able to hone your psychic abilities, your ability to forecast. It is not just you. While a great sales leader possesses the ability to predict what's going to happen before it happens, the only way they master that ability is by teaching their own team to predict what's going to happen before it happens.

As you'll read in Chapter 6, this isn't about optimizing your brain to connect with spirits. It's not some magic formula. It *is* about creating and maintaining a culture where losing is celebrated, accuracy is celebrated, and underpromise/overdeliver is not. The culture of forecasting is also the culture of your fifth core responsibility, which is . . .

5) FUN

Building and delivering a culture where your team not only shows up every day, but they are intrinsically inspired to do their best every day, too. They stay, and when they are with their friends, they talk about how great their job is. When that happens, turnover goes down and your speed to hire goes up. In the 2020's hybrid working environment, optimizing fun could quite possibly be your most important job. *Fun* isn't about rainbows and lollypops. It's about optimizing for all the elements that ensure your team wants to be there, wants to grow, and wants to advocate.

Internalize the Five F's. Your responsibility is to establish and maintain the focus of your optimal targets; build and optimize a field organization based on that focus; ensure that your field organization is doing the fundamentals correctly every time; monitor and measure to predict the future through a forecast; and create a fun environment where that team wants to stay, perform, and advocate.

This framework, once internalized, becomes what you fall back on when the bullets start flying. For your one-on-ones. For your "all hands" meetings. For your board. For your planning. For the way you think about the business on a day-to-day basis.

The following five chapters dig into each one of these F's, with tools and resources you can use to optimize each. Regarding the fifth F, fun, we'll explore that responsibility in an entire section, because nothing happens without an intrinsically inspired team, one filled with P.R.A.I.S.E. The science of engagement is fascinating, and at the same time, the impact of disengagement on sales performance is terrifying.

Without a simple framework, your day-to-day efforts as a sales leader could resemble that dog chasing a car bumper down the road, not knowing where the car is headed. Sales leadership, like sales, requires a structure and process.

You ready? Let's dig into the structure, starting with focus.

CHAPTER 3

FOCUS
FIELD
FUNDAMENTALS
FORECAST
FUN

There are hundreds, perhaps thousands, or even millions of possible patrons whom you might serve so satisfactorily that they would become permanent and profitable, but they have to be sifted out of the great mass whom your business cannot serve.

— Arthur Sheldon, *The Art of Selling*, 1911

NOT ALL CUSTOMERS ARE EQUALLY DESIRABLE.

From the beginning of your tenure as a sales leader, ensuring your team is working on the right opportunities in the right places at the right time is a core responsibility. I often referred to it as a "no science projects" philosophy, centered on the realization that your sales organization's most finite resource is their time.

Who will you say *yes* to? Who will you say *no* to? What criteria will you use for the gray areas in between to make that determination? This must be well defined, frequently reviewed, and adjusted as required.

Our natural inclination seems to be toward selling to anyone interested in buying. However, the focus, when done correctly, optimizes your return on time in such a dramatic way. It can be the difference between success or failure for a leader and, ultimately, for an organization.

It was a new year, and a Chicago-based technology startup was beginning to shift its attention toward building its revenue engine. They had a product that worked. They had a smattering of customers who were not only getting value from the solution but also looking for ways to use it even more.

In looking at their initial customers, there was enough data to configure a theory about who the initial target for their solution should be. We sat down and went through it.

Together, we determined that the focus would be on retailers who sell online. The industries with which we would focus were to be in the general merchandise, apparel, health, and beauty categories. We would only pursue companies headquartered in the United States.

To optimize efforts with minimal available resources, the focus would also be on companies whose annual revenues are larger than $50 million (so they are not too small to drive the purchase volume needed to see the desired impact). These organizations should also be smaller than $1 billion in annual revenues (so they are not so big that they require a super-unique installation, which also requires an expensive selling process).

I asked Jon, their founder/CEO, "What will you do if you receive an inbound lead that doesn't match the criteria?"

He said, "The only gray area is going to be the industry verticals for right now. If an electronics retailer comes along, we'll certainly investigate. However, for the others, given where we are, we're going to have to say *no* for now."

Fantastic.

Two months later, during one of my regular calls with Jon, he couldn't wait to share some "great" news, "Todd, guess what! We received an inbound lead from . . . .wait for it . . . Walmart! They had been considering developing their own solution, but found us while doing a Google search. It's a perfect match."

Yes, the largest retailer in the world, Walmart, had reached annual revenues of over $500 billion.[15]

"Jon, are you sure you want to go after this? Remember our discussion. There were strong reasons why you weren't well positioned to pursue retailers over $1 billion in annual revenues. Walmart is 500 times that," I asked Jon.

With a hint of disappointment based on my not-so-excited response, Jon replied, "Todd, it's Walmart. If we can get them on as a client, everything else will fall into place. We'll have street credibility, which will draw in countless other retailers. That credibility will also aid in our ability to secure investment."

"Be careful," I replied.

"This is all teed up. The initial discussions appear to show that we have already developed the exact solution they were looking for. Off we go!"

Fast-forward six months.

Jon and his team had flown out to their San Bruno, California, offices multiple times to meet with the Walmart team. As a result of those meetings, Jon's product development roadmap had to be rebuilt entirely and prioritized to tightly align with Walmart's requirements. No contracts had been signed yet. Walmart had yet to give Jon's company a single dollar.

It was now September. Jon received a call from Walmart. "Jon, it's been so great getting to know and work with your team. We're locking down for the holiday rush now. All our focus and efforts will be on that, so let's reconnect on this in January. Cool?"

It was now January. Jon noticed on LinkedIn that one of the core team members his organization had been working with at Walmart had changed companies. Another? Changed jobs within Walmart. Nobody was answering the phone when he called in January.

His company was practically on life support, having burned through months of cash, having changed their product roadmap to support this whale instead of their core focus. They had six months to live, before the doors would need to be closed.

Focusing on the wrong opportunities can have catastrophic consequences when it's as strategic a decision as this.

At the rep level, the collection of times we are focused on the wrong opportunities at the wrong time adds up, and without even noticing, can have catastrophic consequences on your team's performance, too.

If you are building out a revenue-getting organization or taking over a new team, the primary asset you have in your inventory is time. Focusing that time on the right opportunities and the right individuals within those opportunities is the first step to optimizing that inventory.

And, as an ongoing responsibility that you have as a leader, establishing, maintaining, adjusting, and analyzing that focus is core.

What are the ideal firmographics (company sizes, verticals, geographies) and demographics (titles, levels) of the companies and individuals within those companies which will grant us the easiest path to the highest reward? Which will we say *yes* to, which will we say *no* to, and what criteria will we use to determine the gray areas?

Jon understood.

Pat, another early-stage CEO, did not. As I sat in Pat's office, I asked, "What will be the focus of your targeting?"

He walked up to his whiteboard and wrote the revenue band which will make up his firmographic focus:

"< $10 million in annual revenue to > $1 billion in annual revenue"

I gazed upon the whiteboard like a confused dog. "Isn't that everyone?" I asked.

"Yes."

If you focus on everything, you are focused on nothing at all.

FOCUS: IT'S DIFFERENT THAN TAM AND ICP

As an organization, you've likely defined your TAM (total addressable market), which is a calculation that theoretically answers this question: If we sold everything we have to every possible company that could derive value from our solutions, what would that dollar amount be? In most cases, that number is a ridiculously high amount. Salesforce.com, whose annual revenues are just over $21 billion through their 2021 fiscal year, reports a TAM of $175 billion.[16]

While a TAM is interesting, what is your optimal addressable market for today? A hunter could state that the total number of birds in a town is 1,000. Thus, their strategy will be just to spray buckshot across the town and see how many they can hit. Not an optimal approach, right? The result would be tons of inefficiency, wasted effort, and unintended consequences.

The majority of organizations next identify what is referred to as an ICP, which stands for an ideal customer profile. The ICP answers the question for investors and potential referrers, "What is the profile of customer that is ideal for your organization? In a perfect world, if you could only work on one type of customer where the mutual impact would be optimal, what would that profile look like?"

Ideal, defined as "satisfying one's conception of what is perfect; most suitable." If you were hot, what would be the ideal means to resolve that issue? Jumping into a pool? To me, that sounds ideal. However, there are many options. You could drink some water, or even a sports drink. You could spray yourself with water. If you're near a grocery store, maybe you could walk into their beer cooler. You could jump into a pond or stand in front of a fan. While those are not all ideal, they will get the job done.

When considering your ICP, is that the way you think about it? "We'll go after anyone with a heartbeat, but our ICP is . . . "

A focus is the establishment of a target *prioritization* within your team. It's clicking even deeper onto your ICP to answer the questions;

- Who will you say *yes* to pursue?
- When will you say *no*?
- What criteria will you use to assess the gray areas, or when to expand your focus?
- When your salespeople wake up in the morning and look at all the targets they could call on, how do they prioritize?

The answer to that final question above should be easy, made easy by you. By doing so, they gain expertise in that area of focus. They gain confidence and optimize their time. And, without even trying, when a concept or area of focus becomes apparent, the phenomenon called Baader-Meinhof kicks in.

Baader-Meinhof, also known as the frequency illusion or frequency bias, once you as a human being establish a focus, it stays top of mind. You notice it everywhere. Our family is considering buying a boat for the first time. As neophytes, we intend to purchase a used boat before getting too crazy. Since it's top of mind, as we drive down the street, it's almost as though boats are everywhere. We see people pulling them, storing them, and selling them. With an established focus within your team, your team will notice things that align with that focus seemingly everywhere as well. We'll discuss this concept more below in the magic of practicing *extreme firmographic focus.*

Establishing a focus is a constantly evolving part of your role as a sales leader. It begins by firmly defining three categories of focus: firmographics, demographics, and prerequisites.

FIRMOGRAPHICS

When considering the targets that represent the most efficient path to the most profitable and sustaining clients, start with firmly identifying the organizations' firmographics that represent your ideal focus. Firmographics are the attributes of the organizations or companies; their sizes, verticals, and geographies.

Company Sizes: What are the key attributes in terms of company size which represent our profitable, efficient, and sustainable clients? Typically, this is measured in organizational revenue, but this metric may be specific to your organization. For example, as I work with organizations that sell to schools, this size metric could be attributed to the number of schools in a district or the number of students. In another company, they target organizations based on their number of employees, and another bases their company size focus on the number of products they sell.

It's important when considering how you will define your firmographic focus and how you will monitor and adjust long term. The metrics you use are easily discernible from the outside: company revenue, number of employees, number of schools or students in a district or university.

Industry Verticals: Are there certain characteristics regarding the industry an organization is in that lend themselves to a direct-hit alignment between our value proposition and their challenges? When we look at our customer base, which verticals have the highest win rate and/or the highest average contract value and/or shortest sales cycle.

In my last role as chief revenue officer of a ratings and reviews technology provider, our focus was on retailers and brands. That's all. Periodically we would receive inquiries from significant organizations outside of that industry focus, and while we did sometimes win those, the metrics told a different story. A cruise line wanted to add ratings and reviews to their website relating to the different cruises and ships.

It was not in our wheelhouse, and the addressable market for cruise lines was small. However, one of our more expensive reps circled resources around it for months, eventually closing a deal below our averages, requiring unfamiliar contractual terms, and they didn't renew after year one.

Geographies: Are there traits relating to the location of these targets which lend themselves to the ideal efficiency metrics? While this could be very specific to regions, states, or even zip codes, at the very least define the country or countries you will say *yes* to.

Even considering my current business speaking and teaching, there are geographies I say *yes* to, but also ones I now know to say *no* to. For example, I live in Chicago. Two years ago, an organization in Brazil reached out to me for a potential speaking gig. I must admit, I got a little endorphin rush from it, thinking, "Wow, that could be cool!" Given the most important asset I have to convert to revenue is my time, I dug in. I quickly found issues with tax policy, import tariffs for sending books, even the process to acquire a work visa to fly down. Hours and hours are gone, for what would have ended up being an unprofitable result. Lesson learned.

As you begin your new leadership role, spend the time to identify the firmographics of the organizations your team should prioritize. During your tenure, an important responsibility will be to not only maintain that focus, but also to consistently consider and adjust that focus as warranted. You will do this at the team level, but also at the individual level during one-on-ones.

One of our enterprise reps ran into my office with the following news, "Hey, Todd, I just qualified a lead with a massive online travel company. They've been doing ratings and reviews manually and want to outsource it!" It's a company you've heard of, however, our focus was solely on retailers and brands. Not travel. Was there a bit of an endorphin rush associated with the opportunity to capture the top online travel site, and the associated revenue along with it? Yes. Did it have the potential to be a massive deal? Sure. Will it be an efficient application of our finite resources? Not likely. In this case, sure enough, my stubbornness of focus was trumped by our overall leadership team's decision. Once in a while I turn out to be right, and this was one of those cases. We wasted four months. We didn't know that space. Our solution didn't align quite perfectly. We lost, lost slowly, and as for the sales rep assigned to handle this massive lead? She left two months later.

EXTREME FIRMOGRAPHIC FOCUS

While this may sound counterintuitive, I am long an advocate for something I like to call "extreme firmographic focus," meaning, find a vertical you can really help and focus on it completely for a predetermined period of time.

In one organization, we were struggling to find momentum. We had a solution ideal for large manufacturing companies across any industry (machinery, oil and gas, automotive, aerospace) and furniture retailers whose customers would have to do their own assembly (think IKEA). In other words, our solution had broad application across different industries, thus a broad ICP. We had just closed a large opportunity with a gigantic airplane manufacturer. The value proposition was a homerun. Easy pricing justification. Smooth differentiated journey. There was something about companies that made airplanes (commercial and defense-focused) that struck a chord. We had a small team, where each salesperson had 200 target accounts, each including a couple of companies across verticals.

While our team could have continued to call on accounts across the broad swath of industries, for the next two months, we rallied the organization to focus specifically on aerospace and defense (A&D). Our marketing team tailored everything to the A&D vertical. We brought in industry experts to teach us the intricacies of the space. We found out what magazines they read and started reading them. The Baader–Meinhof phenomenon was in full effect, where each of us happened to see and notice A&D learnings everywhere we looked. Our confidence grew. Our messaging was refined and elevated.

As discussed in the previous chapter, confidence is contagious. Our expertise oozed from our sellers in the form of credibility to their prospects, and the next thing we knew, our pipeline grew full of highly qualified deals in the A&D vertical. We closed almost all of them. The team's average deal sizes were almost twice what we had been doing previously, which was scattered across industries.

We then expanded that focus out slowly. What learnings could easily get us to another vertical quickly? We went to heavy machinery and automotive next in the East and Midwest territories of the United States (i.e., Caterpillar, John Deere, Ford, and General Motors), while focusing efforts on oil and gas companies in the South (i.e., Halliburton and Schlumberger). There was magic in that approach. We grew 400% year-over-year and set the organization up for a successful exit. Extreme firmographic focus.

Another way to think about it . . .

A senior sales leader with a Chicago tech company called me for some advice. He had a small team covering a large geographical territory. Some of the sales representatives had quite literally a thousand companies they could call on. This was less the result of a lack of focus, and more the result of a lack of resources. His question for me, "How should I establish rules to bring their account list down from 1,000 down to more like 100?"

The traditional answer would be for the sales leader to prioritize the 1,000 for the team, establish generalizations around their traits, then chop the territories—more rules, less accounts, and potentially 900 accounts suddenly left with no owner.

Or, you could instead empower your team through resources and education.

"You each have 1,000 accounts across a bevy of retailers. For the next four weeks, we're going to make you experts in the category of *shoes*. We're going to bring in customers from companies like Crocs, Skechers, and Cole Haan. The marketing team is going to polish up and educate you on our shoe company success stories. We're going to do an ad campaign around the value of our solutions to shoe companies. Here's a list of 10 social media accounts to follow which focus on the vertical . . . "

As a sales representative, which would you prefer? More rules? Or more education and control? Likely the latter, right? As a rep, the opportunity to make me an expert in something, driving me to be more confident when I have those discussions, then choosing the 25 apparel-shoe companies out of my own list to focus on rather than my boss doing it for me? Win, win, win.

Here's how this level of focus looks.

With extreme firmographic focus, you begin by doing the work, research, and measurement on which key subsets of the overall target market are most ripe for opportunity, maximize deal sizes, win rates, and most efficient cycle lengths. Look at the recent deals of substance that you have won. Is there anything in common about those?

Say, for example, you have just won a large transaction with a medical device company, and each of your team members has several medical companies in their territories. Rally your marketing organization around those types of companies. Marketing's focus becomes tuned to medical devices—messaging, case studies, branding. You set up lunch-and-learns or opportunities for your sales team to hear from medical device experts and talk with the company of that type you just won.

Without even telling your team that, "for the next six weeks, prioritize the medical device companies on your list," your team will want to. You've given them tools to use, education, and confidence. You haven't taken anything away from them. You haven't told them they can't call on other prospects in their turf. Instead of more rules and restrictions, you've uplifted the team, given them more control and development. Then watch the magic happen.

After a few weeks of pipeline development and effort in that category, expand out slowly. What other verticals are like medical devices? Which of the lessons we learned over the past six weeks can we easily apply to that next category? As an organization, you'll quickly become the default solution aligned to the focus you have selected. Momentum and confidence will grow, and that confidence is contagious.

DEMOGRAPHICS

Not all individuals within your target companies are equally desirable, either.

As a sales leader, understanding where your team and your organization's focus should be extended to the functions and levels of individuals worth pursuing. And even more important, identifying the individuals *not* worth pursuing.

For example, you have a solution that provides tremendous benefit to finance teams. Serving as Captain Obvious, you clearly want to focus your team on selling to individuals within the finance organization. However, how tightly do you focus your efforts on the levels within a finance organization? Do you have the data around your win rates, deal sizes, and cycle times based on the differences between selling to a chief financial officer versus a corporate controller? An accounting clerk versus a vice president of finance? As a leader, where is your team's focus?

What do you do if an inbound lead comes in from a function or level that doesn't match? Will you pursue them? Will you refer them out?

In my last company, our technology was most tightly aligned to eCommerce teams, those who were responsible for selling things online. Ideally, the higher within the eCommerce function we could get, the better. This isn't the case in all organizations, but for us, a chief digital officer, a vice president of eCommerce, even a director of digital were great for us. However, what happens when we are brought in and/ or relegated to marketing, or someone lower in the digital department like an SEO manager?

Your reps may feel that "If, when I hold a mirror under the prospect's nose, it steams up, they're worth pursuing." You need to know better. Who will you say *yes* to pursuing? Who will you say *no* to pursuing? And for the gray areas, what criteria will you use to make the call?

Even in my speaking and sales training business I run today, this consideration is of the utmost importance. When I receive a reach-out from a leader in sales or in sales enablement, my win rate is incredibly high. My cycle lengths are short. My deal sizes are higher for sales leadership leads versus sales enablement leads, but they are both great. These types of opportunities are the most frequent for my business and are almost always a *yes* in my decision to pursue them.

On the other hand, when I receive an inbound lead from *regional* sales leadership, especially in larger organizations, those opportunities struggle to close. And, when they do, they close for lower dollar amounts. When I come upon one, I then determine whether I can help the regional leader navigate their own organization to connect on a broader level across their organization. If I can't, it becomes a judgment call. A *maybe*.

When a lead comes in from a different department, all bets are off. In those instances, I am likely to do a deeper discovery, and often I refer those to other peers. For example, early in 2020 I had someone in the training-and-development function within human resources reach out. I pursued it because the company was significant. The process was highly involved, requiring much more sales effort on my part. The connection between their issues and my programs were more difficult to explain, as this individual did not have a core comprehension of the sales function. They asked for references. I had never been asked for formal references before. In the end, they went in another direction. I quickly realized that leads from human resources were not the best use of my limited inventory of time, and now when one comes in, I do a quick discovery, and refer them out. Those are a no.

That is your responsibility as a leader: to find the more efficient path to the highest value opportunities in terms of cost of acquisition and profitability. Cost of acquisition and profitability draw a direct line from opportunity flow, deal sizes, win rates, and sales cycle lengths.

PREREQUISITES

The final category in your focus responsibility is to understand the soft or hard prerequisites an organization must have to make it worth pursuing. What are the things a company must have, or must have in place, to make it a valuable opportunity for your team and business?

One of my software clients sells technology that works on any device but is designed for those using an Apple Mac. For clients using a Windows environment, for example, the client would need to install a Mac virtual environment first. When pursuing opportunities, they embrace transparency by leading with an explanation to the client about this focus. "Before we go too far in this discussion, our technology runs natively on a Mac. If you're not a Mac environment, there are two paths we can take. The first is to assess your appetite for establishing a virtual Mac environment on your Windows machines for your users. However, many organizations that are Windows first prefer not to do that, so the second path is to part as friends right now."

This sales organization finds that revealing this concept early builds trust and speeds their path to winning fast when a client is primarily in a Mac environment. Even better, this speeds their path to losing fast, too. If the client is in a Microsoft Windows–only environment, it is likely not worth pursuing for either party.

Take a moment to identify what your team's focus should be. What are the firmographics, demographics, and prerequisites that make for an optimized sale and long-term advocating customer? Who will you say *yes* to, and who will you arm your team to say *no* to? What criteria will you use to make quick decisions on the prospects and customers who fall into the gray area, where their traits are a mix of the *yes* and the *no*. And, when they are a mix, don't be afraid to let the customer decide through transparently sharing the dilemma. Win fast through building trust and aiding the customer to predict, but even more importantly, lose fast the opportunities you are apt to lose eventually.

Yes or No Criteria	
Firmographics (Sizes, geography, vertical, ...)	
Demographics (Individuals, titles, ...)	
Prerequisites (Team, technology, complexity, ...)	

Criteria for the "Maybes"
What are the costs associated with this opportunity? (Opportunity cost? Hard dollar cost?)
What are the market implications of working this opportunity? (New vertical? New geography?)
What else?

The most valuable asset you and your team members have is their time. Your first responsibility, both initially and ongoing, is to establish and maintain your team's focus on the right opportunities at the right time.

While the average sales leader seeks to cast a wide net of potential clients and work every opportunity where the prospect has interest and budget, the world-class sales leaders embrace the idea of "no science projects," and help their team maximize their results through embracing an extreme focus on the ideal pursuits.

CHAPTER 4

FOCUS
FIELD
FUNDAMENTALS
FORECAST
FUN

*A salesperson's territory is like a corn-field. It won't yield
harvest without cultivation. Weeds are the only crop
that will come up of themselves.*

— W. C. Holman, *Ginger Talks*, 1912

I T WAS MY FIRST DAY ADVISING A NEW CHICAGO-BASED CLIENT. THIS WAS
a technology startup focused on the transportation industry. The founder/CEO
greeted me at the door, quickly showed me around, then pointed to the conference room.

"I know we're just getting started, but I have an incredible candidate sitting in there.
How would you feel about popping in, introducing yourself, and maybe doing a
quick interview?"

"For what role?" I asked.

"Sales! She's been in the industry for over 20 years and comes with an incredible Rolodex of contacts," he replied.

The woman in the conference room was a super veteran in the industry. She ran networking events for logistics leaders. She executed large transactions with multiple buyers over long sales cycles. However, sales at this startup did not require that skillset. After honing the organization's focus based on their solution and impact, the transactions we would be doing would be just that . . . transactions. Single buyer, lower budget, fast decision cycles. The interview that was being done with her was for the wrong role. Yes, she could be an incredible asset to the organization, but not as a frontline salesperson.

That mismatch created a misalignment in the interview. This turned out to be a classic example of beginning to build a field organization without knowing what the focus will be. The order between focus and field matters, and it certainly did in this case.

Based on your focus, your next responsibility is in building, maintaining, and growing the field organization, which is putting the right people in the right roles in the right places with right tools and the right resources.

THE RIGHT PEOPLE

Just like salespeople need to always be on the lookout for great prospects, as a sales leader, it's likely you will always be recruiting. The team that takes the field each day will need to be the optimal team to play the game you are playing—your focus. How will you align your search with your focus?

As you will learn later, we as human beings have a series of feelings that drive our level of engagement, comfort, and inspiration. The recruiting process plays a key role in the perception of you and your organization, the expectations of the job, and the potential hiree's ability to predict whether they will find a home with you and your company.

Should you create a formal structure in your interview process? Should you establish consistent processes and questions asked to everyone? Those are two very difficult questions to answer, and I believe the optimal way is somewhere in between.

Interviews that are a free-for-all lend themselves to bias. In a free-for-all interview, we, as human beings, create a first impression of the individual we are interviewing. It's a trait acquired and honed from the beginning of time—when those first impressions were used to keep yourself and your tribe alive. That's good for survival thousands and millions of years ago, but not good for building strong, diverse, optimal teams that align with your focus. We then subconsciously use the interview to reinforce our initial feeling. We lead the individual in the direction of helping us support the argument for moving forward with them. Maybe you switch your own brain into sales mode, where you begin to sell the individual on why this is the right next home for them, instead of truly diagnosing the fit.

Interviews that are highly structured, where the questions are predetermined, and every individual is asked the same questions, creates a different dilemma. A structured interview process includes four core elements: (1) question consistency, (2) evaluation standardization, (3) question sophistication, and (4) rapport building. While it may increase the consistency and validity of the process, our brains seek control. As a candidate, the feeling of a loss of control of the conversation means a loss of control of the impression being created, which increases anxiety, and likely sours the individual on the opportunity itself.[17]

What is one to do?

Determine the key attributes that make a successful team member, based on the required focus. Do your sales pursuits require hunting, farming, or a little bit of both? Will these pursuits be long, highly involved processes where consensus among multiple buyers will be required, or are they short, one-call close-type transactional sales? Think about the solution, the industries, and their ability to acquire and maintain confidence with your customers and prospects.

Below are my favorite 10 questions I liked to ask in my sales position interviews. I never asked all of them, but with each question, I have explained below what I was listening for in the answers provided. These questions are meant to be broad, a touch unpredictable without being cheesy, and create an environment where the individual can show their true self, to control the impression they are creating, while giving me and my team a better feel for their fit.

When you have an experienced rep for the role, your focus is: what intrinsic and extrinsic things can we provide to keep this person motivated, and will they fit in and succeed here? Over the thousands of interviews I've done, I've found this collection allows me to get at the real drivers of engagement, passion, fit for the role, fit with the team, potential longevity, and ultimately mutual success.

Hopefully you can use this: (a) as prep if you're interviewing for a role, or (b) as questions to ask if you're an interviewer to help illuminate what's inside the candidates you are interviewing.

QUESTION 1: TELL ME YOUR STORY.

I know, I know . . . it's not a question. But what I'm looking for is storytelling ability. In a sales capacity, the ability to tell stories that are clear, concise, and memorable (in a positive way) is pretty darn important. How does this individual frame their career? Does this individual know how to communicate in a clear, concise, and compelling way? Are they overly verbose? How do they communicate? This allows me to assess whether this person can sit across the desk, conference room table, Zoom call, or telephone with a client and tell a story that matters. If they are not able to tell their own story, how will they be able to tell a story where the client is the hero?

QUESTION 2: WALK ME THROUGH THE LAST X YEARS OF YOUR RESUME. WHY DID YOU TAKE THE JOBS YOU DID? WHY DID YOU LEAVE?

To begin, look at the individual's resume. Have they been in the same company for a long time, or does their resume bounce around with multiple short stays? I like this question to understand whether an individual is good at discovery.

Salespeople need to be good at doing discovery when they are pursuing sales opportunities, right? Their ability to assess whether an opportunity is a good fit for their investment of time and our organization's deployment of resources is vital to both their performance, and your own as a leader. If there's any time to recognize whether the sales candidate can do a strong discovery, it's by diving into how they do discovery for their own career choices, right? Individuals who take and change jobs often are often considered job hoppers. That's not necessarily a bad thing, but it could be a warning sign.

With this question, I'm listening for: (a) how the individual assessed whether an opportunity was worth committing to, (b) what the individual missed during that assessment, and (c) what the individual learned from each. Does this individual get happy ears? Does this individual blame others for their own inability to have predicted their potential experience? Did this individual do their homework before committing? And when it didn't work out, how did that influence this individual's assessment of the next role?

QUESTION 3: IF YOU WERE PUT IN FRONT OF A ROOM OF 500 RANDOM PEOPLE TO GIVE A TALK, WHAT SUBJECT WOULD YOU KNOW MORE ABOUT THAN ANYONE ELSE IN THE ROOM?

It doesn't matter what the subject of the answer is for this one. I'm assessing what a person is passionate about, and more importantly, is this person *capable* of finding passion for something?

In the process, I also get to learn a little bit about their personality, and maybe even learn something useful myself. I've had some great and unique conversations stem from this question, from one individual's passion and collection for unique neckties, to another's passion for all things NASCAR, while another was the go-to expert amongst her friends in the fine art of gathering and maximizing the value of travel points.

I've had some not-so-good answers more often than one might think, from many people not having anything as an answer to the common, generic answer of "my kids." Well, I would hope you would know more than 500 random people about your kids.

QUESTION 4: WHAT'S YOUR MOST SIGNIFICANT CAREER ACHIEVEMENT?

With this question, I'm trying to understand what the individual is most proud of in their career. Plus, are the situations where the individual derives their pride possible in the environment we are providing? Also important to understand is how this individual goes about setting goals. In other words, was the achievement random, or something the individual focused on attaining? What kinds of things lift their spirits, make them proud, and drive them to achieve even more?

QUESTION 5: FROM WHAT YOU KNOW ABOUT (OUR COMPANY) AND THIS ROLE, WHAT EXCITES YOU MOST ABOUT IT?

The answer to this question screams, "Did you do your homework?" Due to the proliferation of information, reviews, research, articles, blog posts, and social media posts, even the slightest bit of homework will provide a strong answer. You might be surprised at how often the answer to this question is generic, which, for a sales position, is a red flag. How do you feel that the role, company focus, or anything else you found while doing your homework aligns to your passion? What about the role excited you? Is your answer generic or thought out?

QUESTION 6: (FOLLOW-ON TO THE LAST QUESTION) WHAT'S GOING TO STRETCH YOU? MEANING, WHAT DO YOU THINK WILL BE THE GREATEST CHALLENGE YOU WILL FACE HERE?

For starters (and I'm guessing you won't be surprised to hear this), I'm looking for authenticity and transparency from their answers. I'm also looking to understand whether this person is looking to stretch themselves, or just looking for a wheelhouse position that aligns perfectly to their skills. Either one could be fine. Listen for their ability to answer this one beyond the cheesy, traditional "what are your weaknesses" question we were taught to address by spinning a negative into a positive like, "I may just have too much passion for this role." Okay, chief. Simmer down. Their ability to embrace and discuss their passions and their concerns reflects directly with the reality of whether this individual will present our solutions to potential clients as all-things-to-all-people, or can they help sit across the table and mutually decide on fit. Are they desperate for the role, or are they willing to find a well-aligned fit? Fit is important in their careers, but also in aligning solutions with customers.

QUESTION 7: IN YOUR CAREER, WHO HAS BEEN YOUR FAVORITE MANAGER? WHY?

My purpose for asking this question is to provide an understanding of how someone derives engagement from their work. About 70% of engagement is derived directly from an employee's relationship with their manager,[18] so ensuring a culture match is a key element to diagnose prior to hiring.

When I recently hired for my own organization who would be my direct report, I explained, "I don't need to be your favorite, however, I'd like to be near the top." For an individual to commit to your company, and to you as a leader, you certainly do not want misalignment of culture, where they remember you as being one of the worst instead of one of the best. Can you assess the odds of either during the interview process? I believe you can.

QUESTION 8: TELL ME ABOUT A DEAL YOU WERE RESPONSIBLE FOR THAT YOU'RE PARTICULARLY PROUD OF? HOW DID YOU DEVELOP IT?

Depending on the role I'm interviewing for, what about the deal they are most proud of do they take pride in? Look for when they light up during the story. Are those types of opportunities even possible here? Does the opportunity described in any way match the role you are seeking to fill? For example, does their source of pride come from the hunt, meaning the pursuit of the new opportunity? Or does it come from the farming, meaning the development of the existing opportunity or account? Was there something special about the sales process itself, meaning the build from taking the opportunity to not recognizing their status quo could use a change all the way to close? The close itself? Something lucky?

QUESTION 9: WHAT IS THE VALUE PROPOSITION OF YOUR CURRENT (OR LAST) COMPANY? HOW WOULD YOU DESCRIBE WHAT THEY DO?

Do you understand their explanation? Do you think you could take the candidate's answer and relay it to a random family member in an understandable way? In a consensus sale, value propositions must be clear, memorable, and easily passed along. Does this person truly understand what they've been selling, and are they able to articulate it in a way that makes sense to the layperson?

QUESTION 10A: WHAT KINDS OF THINGS DO YOU DO TO IMPROVE YOUR SELLING SKILLS?

I've literally had salespeople tell me answers like: (a) "I learn by doing" and (b) "I took a course back with my first job, and that has served me well." You don't need me to tell you this . . . the world of sales is evolving at an accelerating pace. The most successful people (in general) take pride in their profession and are constantly looking for ways to extend their lead. They read, they listen to podcasts, they take classes, they participate in sales communities—they take pride in their career. Given my passion for learning, non-answers to this question typically result in a candidate pass. In some cases, I learn new avenues for my own professional growth through asking this question. Often, it also gives me an indication of their perception of their responsibility as a salesperson, their philosophy and their approach, which leads to question 10b below. If the answer isn't clear from 10a, ask . . .

QUESTION 10B: WHAT IS THE SALES METHODOLOGY/PHILOSOPHY/APPROACH THAT YOU MOST IDENTIFY WITH AND WHY?

This question often gives me a sense for the truth to question 10a above. Does this individual have a framework for their approach? Do they think about their profession like a pilot, ensuring they're always guiding the buyer along their journey without missing key steps? Or are they a fast-food drive-through attendant, there to be nice, maybe try to upsell to a combo meal, but there to take orders?

SIDE NOTE: Now, you may call me old-school, but you know what drives me crazy? Someone who shows up for an interview with nothing to take notes with. I know that an interview is like a date—it's a mutual assessment of fit. However, part of my assessment of your fit is your ability to listen and retain. Because, in front of a potential client, those are two important qualities. And, knowing how the human brain operates, if I'm sharing all sorts of goodness about the organization, team, and role, I'm hoping that, like on a sales call, you'll be able to show me that you've got it! It should be obvious in a virtual meeting or face-to-face whether the individual is taking notes.

TOOLS AND TECHNOLOGY

We appear to be amid a "sales stack" revolution. The sales stack, a term used to represent the "stack" of sales software that a team uses to optimally perform their role, has become a hot topic given the hundreds of technologies now available. Charts displaying every logo for every sales technology tool and resource available on the market are now so plentiful that the charts are nearly illegible. As leaders, we have many tools to support your sales team's efforts around prospecting, engagement, productivity, training, sales intelligence tools, pipeline, forecasting and analytics, calendaring, conversation intelligence, chat, auto dialers, and so on.

It is said that, because of sales technology, the sales profession will change dramatically in the next 10 years. It is also said that those who do not know history are doomed to repeat it.

Let's step back in time together for a moment. It was the second week of July 1916. The World Sales Congress was taking place in Detroit, Michigan.[19] The first of its kind, this conference was attended by 3,000 people associated with the sales profession, with talks from dignitaries from business, renowned sales experts, and even politicians. The theme was "Business Betterment throughout Betterment in Salesmanship," with an aim to "elevate the salesman to a higher plane and emphasize the ethics of salesmanship" and "adopting standards of practice depending on strict business honesty."

The primary keynote speaker? None other than the sitting President of the United States of America, Woodrow Wilson. Think about a sales conference today. The president as the keynote speaker? Seems quite strange, doesn't it? Add to it, in July of 1916, there was a world war raging around the globe, and the United States was on the edge of joining the battle.

Why would a sitting president speak at a conference full of salespeople, in the middle of a world war? Because our country was depending on salespeople! The Industrial Revolution was in full swing. If the United States was to come out on top, it had to be through salespeople—bringing the right products to the right companies at the right time. The president was speaking at such an important conference because the sales profession was one with a mission, putting the customer first for the good of all.

The sales profession was trusted, respected, and even admired in the early 1900s.

What happened? Technology happened. Its misuse devolved the profession back to its deplorable reputation which permeated the late 1800s. There's a tremendous lesson to be learned for current-day salespeople around how to think about the application of technology with our sales teams. Here's the story: Back in the early 20th century, to make a sale, it required a face-to-face interaction. While the telephone had been invented, it wasn't until the 1950s that it became more pervasive in the sales world. There was no email or Zoom. You could send a letter, and retailers were using mail order catalogs to secure sales, but real sales were done in person, human-to-human. It was the only way.

As the late 1920s arrived, the economy was turning for the worse. The Great Depression drove sellers into a me-first mode, which was certainly understandable. But what about afterwards?

The greatest "sales stack" revolution of all time happened. While you might consider call recording, list building, or enablement tools to be a revolution, what about the proliferation of the telephone? Would you not consider it to be the greatest game changer in the history of sales? No longer did we need to leave the office to connect with prospects. With the phone, sellers who could only visit a few prospects per day could now communicate over wires directly to as many as they could call in a day!

But we ruined it.

Unwanted generic pitches. Metrics and call targets incentivizing *quantity* over *quality*. Aggressive tactics. Auto dialers. Robocalls. The sales professional's usage of the greatest gift to date given to the sales world required an entire industry of technologies needing to be created to prevent salespeople's misuse of it. Dr. Shirley Jackson's inventions led to the creation of caller ID.[20] Then came answering machines and voice mail. Call blocking tools that you are probably using right now.

Call prevention technologies weren't enough. The government had to step in, creating legislation including the "Do Not Call Registry" in 2003. According to the Federal Trade Commission, the sales problem is so bad that there are currently 221 million phone numbers on the list.[21]

Then came the sales professionals' next great gift, email. The incredible ability to communicate electronically, to send a message and have it instantly appear in the mailbox of the intended recipient. What an incredible, game-changing gift to the sales profession.

But we ruined it.

Generic spam messages, unrelenting reach outs, scams, and trickery made email the next target of even more technology innovations. Solutions from tools to recognize unwanted messages to IP blacklists and inbox wizards developed and designed to restrict salespeople and send those messages to junk and spam folders.

Those email sales-prevention strategies weren't enough, either. And, once again, the government had to step in, creating legislation through the 2003 CAN-SPAM Act,[22] which made opt-ins and unsubscribe links a requirement to make swatting away salespeople easier.

The five-letter dirty word is S-C-A-L-E. Sales leaders and organizations prioritizing volume over quality, relationships, and focus. The great gifts of technology sullied by our forgetting that we're selling to human beings. We stopped seeing our customer's eyes, and instead only focused our sight on our own metrics.

The great gifts kept coming. Just prior to the signing of the CAN-SPAM Act, LinkedIn began—an incredible gift for salespeople, where hyper-targeting became possible. As a salesperson, you could now see a person's picture, title, their entire resume, location, interests, and posts before ever reaching out. We've also been given the gift of video, enabling salespeople to send conversations beyond just words. In each case, salespeople have tried to ruin them through scale.

So, how do we regain our respect? You must be trusted to be respected. Trust and respect require a shift back to humanness in our profession. It requires a shift back to ensuring our customers and prospects truly believe we care about their outcomes, not just our bank accounts.

The best way to make a customer and/or prospect believe we truly care about their outcomes is to truly care about their outcomes. The decisions you make as a sales leader around what tools and technology to invest in must come from a customer-outcome perspective. It's up to you to decide whether you want technology to take your team and the sales profession forward or backwards.

Build, maintain, and grow your field organization to best serve the focus, not the other way around.

CHAPTER 5

FOCUS
FIELD
FUNDAMENTALS
FORECAST
FUN

Who expects or demands results of the physician, lawyer,
engineer or any other important worker, without long,
arduous training? Why this seeming exception in the case of
the sales professional?

— B. C. Bean of the Shaw-Walker Co., 1905

N EARLY 2011, I JOINED A COMPANY CALLED EXACTTARGET. I WAS TASKED
with running one of North America's four "New Business" regions. New hires into
the organization were required to attend a week of what was called NEO (new
employee orientation), followed by a two-week program for salespeople called
NEST (new employee sales training).

The NEO program was fantastic. We'll discuss an element of the program later and
how it instilled a firm foundation of true empathy into every employee while also
contributing to the company's culture.

However, before attending the two-week NEST program, my boss warned me, "Todd, just know that *we know* the NEST program is not optimal. Resist the urge to get frustrated, or even worse, resist the urge to just stand up and take it over."

I maintained my composure for a total of three days. By Thursday morning of the first week, my attention shifted from attempting to consume and digest the content to instead thinking about the delivery of the content. In my new role, I would be hiring salespeople. If my new salespeople attended this program, I felt as though I would still have a lot of work to do once they had completed it.

In a momentary lapse of control, I did take over part of a session on that fourth day of NEST. By that Thursday morning, the realization hit me that the group of individuals taking the class with me were not getting up to speed the way they should. It did not adhere to the way the human brain prioritizes their attention, absorbs content, and, fundamentally, it did not adhere to the way we learn. It was nobody's fault. It reflected what had always been done, not just at ExactTarget, but across the sales profession in general.

I subdued my urge for the remaining program; instead, I arduously began to take notes. I shared my ideas with my boss following the program, then dug into my own responsibilities of building, growing, and leading my team.

Eight months later, I walked into a conference room in our Indianapolis headquarters. In the room sat our chief operating officer, our senior vice president of field operations, and the woman who had been running NEST.

"Todd, we want you to rebuild our sales enablement function. Tear it down to the studs and build it up the way you want to build it." We would soon be hiring between 20–30 new individuals into the sales organization per month. Onboarding had to be done right, and the organization was willing to maintain my compensation level. Apparently, the notes I had taken and shared following my experience through the program stuck.

I was all in. This was my nerdery. However, the first thing I did after leaving the meeting was to open my laptop and Google, "sales enablement." At the time, the term "sales enablement" was relatively new. Was it sales training, or something broader?

I sought to leverage my experiences as a sales nerd, combining my love of learning science with my love of sales philosophy, and build out a program like no other. I was able to put together a team, learn from the greatest thought leaders in the education space, and make the right investments, and they served us well. We scaled at an incredible clip, had a successful IPO, then got acquired by Salesforce.com for $2.7 billion. I played a very small role in the overall outcome, but the structure of how you consider solidifying the fundamentals really matters to your ability to grow and scale an organization.

The build of enablement mattered. It mattered in our ability to rally sales leadership to maximize the investments in new and existing hires. It kept turnover low. It allowed us to drive better alignment to the company's culture. And, once we were acquired by Salesforce and a guy named Mark Benioff asked, "Who is going to teach our 2,000 salespeople what we just spent almost $3 billion on?" the answer was my team. And because we built it right and built it to scale, we were able to accomplish Benioff's target (aka, ultimatum) in under six weeks.

While that may not be your story, your third ongoing sales leadership function is to drive the fundamentals that maximize the field's effectiveness. Defining and now driving your team's focus on the right opportunities at the right time, building a team to take the field filled with the right people in the right roles in the right places, with the right tools and the right resources is just the start. Now they must execute, and you must ensure that execution is aligned around the right fundamentals, imparted in the most efficient and effective way possible.

The word *fundamentals* is used on purpose. These are the central principles of which consistent execution is founded. You have a responsibility to ensure that your team members are executing consistently optimal, the right execution in the right situations.

On a regular and ongoing basis, spend the time to break down each of the fundamental elements of a consistent performer.

THE THINGS WE MUST GET RIGHT

What are fundamentals? The fundamentals are the simple things we must get consistently right. These are the 100-level skills. At a high level, it's categories like:

Messaging: Are we consistently messaging to prospects and customers correctly?

Prospecting: How effective are we at inspiring the interest and engagement of our focus targets?

Discovery/Qualification: How good are we at identifying the fit for both the potential customer and our organization?

Presenting: In the more formal engagements with prospects and customers, how are we at maximizing audience engagement, driving action, telling stories, and leading *to* our solution instead of *with* it?

Negotiating: Do we overdiscount? Do we erode trust at the goal line of our deals using techniques taught in hostage negotiation classes? Are we exuding pricing integrity?

How about **sales process execution**? **Hand-offs** to post sales—the team that executes the transaction, the team that cares for the customer longer term? **Deal strategy**?

Start with the basics. As a sales leader, just going through a simple self-scoring of your team is a good place to start. You can use an easy chart like this below or create one that is more specific to your team. If you're leading leaders, have those leaders periodically assess their teams, then consolidate what you find so you can prioritize the investments you make in the fundamentals.

Category	Score	Assessment
Messaging		
Discovery/ Qualification		
Prospecting		
Presenting		
Negotiating		

Let's double-click on a couple of these fundamentals.

Messaging: If you were to ask five members of the team the following question, how would they do in answering it?

You go to a party. You run into a few friends you haven't seen in a while, who are also in the business world. One asks, "Hey, I heard you got a new job. XYZ Company? What do they do?" How would you answer this question so that the listeners would understand it, be able to relate with it, and remember it?

I tried this once with five team members while I was the chief revenue officer at PowerReviews. A generic, bad answer sounds like this, "We sell software." Another bad answer? The bag-o-jargon: "We are obsessed with empowering consumers and corporations with authentic, user-generated content to make better decisions that grow their businesses . . . and their lives!"

A good answer? "At our core, we help retailers and brands collect and display ratings and reviews on their websites. When you buy something online from a retailer, you click on the product, then scroll down to read the reviews. We are often the engine behind the collection and display that you interact with."

So now, whenever you read a review on a retailer's website before buying something, you might think, "I wonder if that's PowerReviews." That's the goal.

Good answers are consistent, relatable, and do not make us the hero.

Think about messaging encompassing not only your positioning but also your delivery, both voice-to-voice and in the written word.

Prospecting: How would you assess your team's ability to engage with your focus targets, drive their engagement, and lead them into a buying process? Are they "we-ing" all over the prospects? Are they eroding trust before they've built any to begin with?

Discovery and Qualification: How would you assess your team's ability to do proper, effective discovery and qualification?

Understand how your team qualifies a prospect. Is your team diagnosing whether there's alignment with your focus? Has the team done its homework before engaging in discovery? A good metric to start thinking about is, for the deals we lose, how long does it take us to lose it and move on? We will lose deals, but what percentage of our time are we spending on opportunities we should have known we were going to lose?

Does your discovery process make a prospect feel like they've been put on the witness stand? Does it feel like the team's questions are focused on helping sell more effectively, or will they truly aid the prospect in their journey? Are the questions self-serving or prospect-serving?

Presenting: I have a lot of opinions on how formal presentations are configured and delivered. There's a chapter on it in *The Transparency Sale*. But for you as a leader, there are two things I want you to consider when assessing the choreography and execution of your presentations:

1. Do our presentations lead *to* us, or do they lead *with* us?
2. Do our presentations offer a collection of logic, or do they tell a story where the prospect/customer is the hero?

Logic is polarizing to the human brain. Think about it. Has a social media post changed your opinion on anything? Probably not. The same dynamic happens in presentations. Presenting logic to someone who already is leaning in a direction—either toward you, away from you, or potentially to the do-nothing status quo, your logic will be used to support that leaning. It will not change it.

The traditional choreography of a presentation drives polarization. It runs 180-degrees from how people come together in an audience. What brings people together? Stories. And given that our presentations are meant to build consensus amongst multiple buyers, telling a story where your customer is the center brings an audience together.

Keep in mind, "Power is neither good nor evil—but its user makes it so."[23] Make sure you use the power of stories for good. Make sure the stories you and your team tell are non-fiction and not "based on a true story."

Negotiating: When you look across the deals you've done, how do you feel about your team's ability to build trust through to the close? Are they building trust or eroding it? How do you feel about your team's ability to maintain pricing integrity, and not just give things away in the form of a discount, resulting in a charitable contribution to the prospect's bottom line?

Negotiating a sale doesn't have to mimic the negotiation of the release of hostages from a bank heist. You can get value for every dollar you give away in the form of a discount. Are you? You can build trust versus eroding it. Are you?

Some of the old-school approaches to driving deal urgency ironically do the opposite. So, as a little fundamentals bonus, here's an idea that will drive deal values, deal urgency, and build trust right through to the goal line.

As a sales leader, it felt like I was giving my sellers a gift when I'd work with my CEO and CFO to get approval to offer a quarter-end discount to our prospects. I was doing the opposite. Given that we weren't just selling transactional deals, but more complex enterprise transactions, the earlier we could establish the promotion, the better.

"Great news! You can start to socialize this with your opportunities right now . . . we'll be offering 10% off for ClosedWon new business signed by the end of the quarter!"

The reps then begin to socialize the promotion with their prospects. As a result, the prospects have now been subconsciously signaled to wait. Think about it from the buyer's lens:

1) "Hmmm, if they're giving me free money now, it'll only get better if we wait to ink this, right?"

. . . so the buyer has been signaled to WAIT.

2) "If they're giving discounts for free now, they just moved the bar from which we'll be asking for more."

. . . so the deal's value has already been eroded, and will be eroded more.

And what does waiting do? Creates more risk in your deal . . .

- Other priorities could sneak in.
- Other options could sneak in.
- Your buyer could decide to leave the company, which seems to be a rampant problem right now.

Any or all of these risks caused by the expiring discount can cause your deal to go . . . *poof* . . . and disappear.

Think about it. If you want to buy something in mid-November, like a new sweater, gaming system, or television, wouldn't it make sense to wait for Black Friday or Cyber Monday? You're ready to buy. But you'd be flushing money by not waiting two weeks.

Once you give something without asking, you've signaled the buyer to ask. Imagine stumbling over a rock and finding a $20 bill under it. Wouldn't you start kicking over every rock? You wouldn't bother if you hadn't accidentally discovered the first one, right?

There is a way to change this dynamic. It takes a little foundation laying and forethought, but it can be done, and has successfully been done in (shameless self-promotion) the companies I've taught transparent negotiations to:

- Step 1: Stop offering expiring discounts. They don't motivate; they decelerate and disintegrate.
- Step 2: Align around the prospect's timing. Discuss a close plan, or as I describe in *The Transparency Sale*, a "mutual decision plan."
- Step 3: Have them put a little skin in the game.

How does this sound?

"There is value to us and our organization in our ability to predict our business. As you can imagine, our ability to forecast impacts every element of our business and us personally in the sales organization."

"If you are willing to mutually align around the timing of when you think you'll get this done, we're willing to pay you in the form of a discount to stick to it."

Have the client tell you when they think it can get done. Add a little buffer. Be transparent.

"So, it appears as though the end of November seems like reasonable timing, right? How about this, if you're willing to help us forecast by getting this done before the holidays . . . so say December 15, as I mentioned before, there's value in our ability to forecast, and value in not having to worry about this in late December. We're willing to pay you in the form of a discount to get this inked and kicked off by December 15. Would that work for you?"

Mutual alignment. Skin in the game for the client. Nothing is given without something received.

And, the transparency of forecast accuracy—an actual explanation for why we'd be willing to pay the prospect in the form of a discount—begets transparency on behalf of the prospect. Of course, you will have instances where the client doesn't get it done in time. I discuss what to do in these instances in the book *The Transparency Sale* and in the Transparent Negotiation workshops.

However, this shift in dialogue and mutual alignment with your prospects will immediately change the discussion and dynamic. It changes the client's motivation. It creates a more accurate forecast. It spreads out your business beyond just the last week of a quarter. It helps you maintain overall deal values. The impact on your own credibility as a sales leader is profound.

And, as a transparency nerd, it helps you build trust through to the goal line versus the traditional approach that erodes it. As a sales leader, you have a tremendous opportunity to teach your reps fundamentals like this which add money in their pocket, skills in their brains, and respect for you. We're more likely to run behind someone who teaches us, builds us up, and lines us up with our desired career path. Take the time to learn fundamentals as a sales leader. Go beyond the forecast in your leadership.

Sales Process Execution: For as much as my kids wanted ice cream, not even they wanted to wait in the long line that greeted us when we got there.

"Can we just go home?" my nine-year-old daughter asked. My eight-year-old son quickly agreed. We were happy to oblige, seeing how many people on the other side of the building were in a holding area waiting for their orders. Five minutes earlier, they had been sooo excited about the ice cream trip.

Either way, it still would have tasted the same—long line or short line. But we all opted out. We all opted for our status quo. We've all done this. We can't find something we're looking for at the giant hardware store, can't find anyone to ask, and just leave the store without it. We arrive at a restaurant without a reservation and see people waiting outside. We keep driving and find somewhere else to go.

We wanted something, we started acquiring that something, and we opted out. We opted for the status quo.

In the business-to-business world, our prospects do this every day. They get excited about a solution. In some cases, they even filled out our lead form, so they must be excited. Then our team engages, and the next thing you know, the opportunity disappears from our pipelines, opting for the status quo or the inferior competitor.

"The prospect suddenly decided to push off this purchase. I don't get it. They were so excited!"

What happened? It goes back to the process.

The reward doesn't look as sweet when the journey to get there doesn't match our expectations. Our brains stack the deck toward the easier path when deciding.

As salespeople and selling organizations, how do we ruin the prospect's excitement for our ice cream? How are we stacking the deck against us? It starts with friction in the journey we take our prospects and buyers through.

As a sales leader, you have everything to do with evaluating and optimizing the sales process. When a prospect engages, there's a level of excitement and curiosity to come with it. With each engagement with you that doesn't follow a logical path and doesn't match expectations, excitement and curiosity wane. How your team executes each of these fundamentals—from their messaging and positioning through negotiations—and even the structure of the contract you give the prospect, contributes to your status quo losses.

Put yourself in the buyer's shoes. When would you have opted out? When would you have decided that *the line is too long—this isn't worth the effort* and begin prioritizing other things?

THE THREE FUNCTIONS OF SALES ENABLEMENT

The concept of sales enablement will be present whether you have the function in your business or not. While the determination of resources more aptly belongs in the category of field, discussed in the previous chapter, the application falls squarely here in fundamentals.

What is sales enablement, and how should you think about it? As pervasive as the function of sales enablement appears to be today, confusion persists at senior levels as to its function, focus, and responsibility.

Sales enablement, as a function, is not sales training. This eye-opening realization must be recognized right away. Instead, sales enablement has three primary and essential responsibilities. If done right, the return on investment (ROI) for sales enablement is infinite. And, if thought about in the right way, approaching the responsibility with a framework for its function will help everyone maintain their sanity. To do sales enablement right, those three primary and essential responsibilities are: (1) amalgamate, (2) orchestrate, and (3) evaluate.

AMALGAMATE

In the B2B space, salespeople continue to represent either the success or failure of their company. They are your organization's voice to the prospect. When words are leaving their larynx, those words represent you. If those words don't properly represent what the company represents, the company will fail. You could have the most fantastic products in the world. Your sellers can still screw that up. The economy could be suffering, causing your organization to be experiencing suboptimal economic conditions. However, your sellers can still succeed.

As a result, every department in an organization wants to *enable* salespeople. Beyond the sales department itself, your *marketing team* wants to enable salespeople. The alignment between a sales and marketing organization is vital to your success, and marketers know it. They need time to teach positioning, lead qualification, and processes; and to work on upcoming events, branding, and so on.

Your product team probably wants to enable salespeople, too. They want to gain alignment to ensure salespeople are aware of current and future product features and functions, roadmaps, and gotchas. Your client success team wants to enable salespeople with: what's working, what isn't, setting proper expectations, and hand-offs and processes. Your finance team wants to enable salespeople through: expense policies, legal requirements, and sometimes even stock option plans and compensation intricacies. Your human resource team wants to enable salespeople on: values, onboarding, and workplace-required training like harassment prevention.

Name any function in a business. There's probably a time when that department wants to enable the sales team. A great sales enablement function's first and ongoing responsibility is to amalgamate those requests, vet them cross-functionally, and then prioritize.

First, establish an initial list of the requirements salespeople must have to be effective and efficient in their roles. Collect those across functions. Meet with your team, your peers, individuals in other departments, and collect their perspectives on what the sales organization must learn and communicate to be successful.

Categorize those into four areas:

1. Sales skills
2. Product knowledge
3. Business/industry acumen
4. General company policies, processes, and requirements

Second, establish the priorities. What are the most important to least important items on the list? Then, establish buy-in from others in the organization. Recognize that every company has hundreds of things that could be taught, but the bandwidth to only do a few. The sales brain only can take on so much, and sellers' most valuable inventory is their time, so be prepared to justify why certain things are a lower priority.

Once in place, the third step is establishing those priorities as the mantra for sales enablement. Because, in short order, someone from somewhere will raise their hand and proclaim something that's not on the list as important. Your sales enablement function must be armed with a way to say, with your backing as a sales leader, "Okay. However, for us to do this request, one of these priorities on the current list needs to be moved down. Which one is it going to be?"

ORCHESTRATE

By definition, *orchestrate* means "to arrange, organize, or build up for special or maximum effect."[24]

Sales enablement is the conductor. Sales enablement determines the optimal path for delivery to produce the optimal outcome.

Based on the desired outcome:

- What is the right format for delivery? Classroom? On-demand course? One-on-one coaching? A guide? Self-guided reading followed by a quiz? An email? A video?
- Who should deliver it? Me? A subject matter expert? An external resource?

Within the orchestration, it is also your responsibility to ensure that you optimize the delivery for how individuals pay attention, engage, consume, and ultimately learn and consolidate.

EVALUATE

The third category of responsibility for your enablement function is to *evaluate*; to assess the effectiveness and success of delivering the priority.

This responsibility focuses on the quantifiable measurement of enablement. This function also helps you see issues before anyone else in an organization. Through the sales enablement function, you have a stronger grasp as to whether an individual on your sales team is going to make it or not. The enablement leader can see the issues with engagement, absorption, alignment, and delivery before anyone else.

For example, you have a new hire going through an onboarding process. Imagine the new hire spending their time doing just that. They're not in the field with their manager or even with prospects and customers. They're likely spending their time with your enablement team and other onboarding peers. Now imagine this new hire doesn't fit the culture, isn't engaging fully with the process, or is simply unable to learn successfully. The sales enabler can see the gap between goal and reality; the sales enabler is also most likely to see it first.

Your sales enablers should be solicited for feedback regularly and enabled to recognize the issues before they hit the field.

Before clouding yourself with the metrics, using them as justification for additional enablement hires or the success of the current, existing team, keep the following in mind: with the number of open sales roles available far exceeding the supply, I believe you cannot invest in sales enablement enough. To hit your targets, hire below the normal bar of requirements and invest in those new hires. Otherwise, you'll be searching for talent that is either: (a) in high demand, or (b) doesn't exist.

Invest in enablement. Invest in the fundamentals. Enablement is an investment, not a cost. Earlier in my career, I thought the opposite, which was a mistake. With limited dollars in a budget, is it easier to invest in resources for whom you can draw a direct line to a return? Or is it easier to invest in resources that make others generate more revenue, but for whom that result is difficult to measure? In an environment where the demand for sales talent so exceeds the supply, you'll find yourself needing to cross out lines on your job description requirements, hire lower, and invest. When things turn around, and the demand balances the supply, simply do the math. Investing in lifting each team member's skillset by even a small percentage has massive results.

The sales profession does not have to be that hard. However, your attention to how your team consistently executes the fundamentals makes all the difference in your attempts to achieve, grow, and scale the right way.

Let's move to the next F, forecast, where (amongst other things) we dive into the math which will not only help you justify the enablement investment but generate many other rewards for you as the sales leader.

CHAPTER 6

FOCUS
FIELD
FUNDAMENTALS
FORECAST
FUN

*If there were no such thing as honesty in the world, we would
have to invent it as an efficiency measure.*

— Glen Buck of Ford Motor Company, 1921

WE ARE TO YOUR FOURTH CATEGORY OF RESPONSIBILITY, THE REQUIRE-
ment of a sales leader to be able to harness the team's ability to predict the
future through an accurate forecast.

Sales forecasting is traditionally fraught with inaccuracy. The subject of
accurate sales forecasting has filled the pages of books, magazines, LinkedIn posts,
and podcast episodes. Yet, tradition reigns. Tradition subconsciously leads to decep-
tion, ultimately resulting in the quarterly surprise against anticipated performance.

In my last role, I was rebuilding a sales organization from the ground up, so I was blessed with the opportunity to create my own rules, test my theories, and build a foundation versus plugging the existing holes. We did things considerably different from tradition regarding forecasting and pipeline. The results? Our sales team achieved within 3.5% of our 90-day forecast for six quarters in a row. In one quarter, we almost hit a 7-figure forecast exactly, filled with both long-cycle-large and short-cycle-small deals (we were off by $12,000).

How? Well, some of it had to be luck. Our run of accuracy was crazy when you think about it. However, there were five ways we bucked traditional approaches to driving a forecast, which, when put together, can't help but drive forecasting breakthrough:

1. We rethought traditional forecast stages and milestones.
2. We rethought traditional qualification criteria.
3. We celebrated the wins and the losses.
4. We eliminated the word *commit* from our vocabulary.
5. We rethought traditional key performance indicators.

1) RETHINKING TRADITIONAL FORECAST STAGES AND MILESTONES

When you look at the forecast stages in your CRM system, the stages that indicate where specific deals are along the process, are they based on what the *seller* is doing, or what the *buyer* is doing? Here are the six typical out-of-the-box stages that come with your CRM system:

- Discovery (5%)
- Qualification (10%)
- Demonstration (25%)
- Presentation (50%)
- Proposal Sent (75%)
- Contract Sent (90%)

It is often said that sales is about guiding the buyer through their purchasing journey to make the best decision for them—as an individual and as an organization.

However, tradition has created a systemic focus for sellers on the achievement of their own milestones. Each traditional stage name listed above is an activity the *seller* is doing. Each word above is rewarding a salesperson's subconscious dopamine system for driving qualified deals through a pipeline based on what the *seller* is doing.

Ironic, given that the point of a forecast is to predict when the *buyer* will sign, and for how much!

While those selling activities may align to a process, the benefit of having sales stages that alert and reinforce a salesperson's need to learn to recognize buyer states and buyer behaviors pays huge dividends in forecast accuracy and overall sales performance. In other words, can you replace existing stage names with the correlating buyer behaviors that drive buyer decision-making progression?

As discussed in Chapter 4 of *The Transparency Sale*, a buyer progresses through three stages on their path to purchase. Consider anything you've purchased of substance. You likely went through a subconscious process of deciding, "Why is my status quo, without this purchase, worth changing?", then "Okay, what solution should I purchase to change my status quo?", and finally, "Do I need to do this right now, or can it wait?" While one could argue the order, the order is quite clear from a forecasting perspective.

1. A buyer first decides "Why change?" Is their status quo no longer sustainable? Do they recognize the need to do something different tomorrow than today? What language have they used to communicate that desire to change? How do their actions reflect that realization?

2. Once the buyer embraces their need to change, they then move on to the question of "Why you?" Recognizing the need to do something different, the client next decides what different looks like. Are you on the short list? Are the buyer activities focused now on your particulars versus an alternative? How many alternatives?

3. After you have been able to confirm that your solution is the chosen path to change, the final step from a forecasting perspective is "Why now?" Every organization has challenges to be addressed. In most cases, they may have hundreds of challenges, with the capacity and resources to address only a tiny percentage of them at a time. Has the client mutually aligned with you on their timing? Are they working through the formalization of the relationship with you with a timing goal?

2) RETHINKING TRADITIONAL OPPORTUNITY QUALIFICATION

What is your favorite movie centering around the sales profession? That question is often asked on LinkedIn posts or during meeting icebreakers. There are not many sales-focused movies to choose from and, while my answer is always *Tommy Boy*, the answers typically include *Boiler Room*, the *Wolf of Wall Street*, and *Glengarry Glen Ross*.

In each of the three movies, the profession is presented as aggressive, dirty, and slimy. The seller is the assassin. The buyer is the targeted victim.

The most famous scene from the movie *Glengarry Glen Ross* occurs when Blake (played by Alec Baldwin) is sent from the headquarters of Mitch & Murray to address the company's branch office sales team. He delivers a verbally abusive speech, at one point flipping the chalkboard to reveal a formula. A-I-D-A. If you have never seen it and would like to, you can easily find that scene on YouTube.

A-I-D-A is described as the stages a buyer goes through: attention, interest, decision, action. Blake and the writers of *Glengarry Glen Ross* did not make up that acronym. It was the basis for how the sales profession thought about sales process and ongoing buyer qualification starting way back in 1898. Elias St. Elmo Lewis theorized AIDA to explain the sequence a buyer goes through to make a purchase. The journey forms a linear hierarchy: is the client interested enough to pay attention, and do they have sufficient desire to act.

In his 1924 book *Salesmanship*, Elmer Ellsworth Ferris not only has AIDA in the core chart (figure below) explaining the sales process, he also goes on to state that "all writers on salesmanship concede that in every sale the mind of the customer will pass through four different stages; attention, interest, desire, and action."

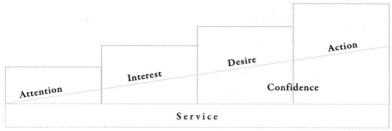

Figure 1 - The Sales Process and Its Basis

During the dawn of professional sales, as Ferris states, everyone knows how buyers will behave, and it's our job to drive them through that journey. The point?

Arthur Sheldon, who I believe to be the G.O.A.T. (greatest of all time) thought leader in sales, sums up the buyer-focused sentiment successful sellers need to have in his 1911 book, *The Art of Selling*:

> *Those people who make the largest fortunes in trade are the people who give most thought to the needs of the public and to the best means of serving them. True salesmanship is the science of service.*

He adds,

> *Now the buyer has a viewpoint, too, and we ought to look at a sales transaction through his eyes. However keen the sellers of today are on making money, the buyer himself is keen on dealing only with those who serve him best.*[25]

As gross as Blake's portrayal of the sales world is in the movie, there is one thing he got right. When we focus our salespeople on recognizing *buyer behavior* instead of focusing our stages on what they, as salespeople, should be doing, our ability to predict when the customer will act changes immediately.

This mindset shift begins with how we think about deal qualification. Start with recognizing a buyer's perspective. Where is the buyer in their journey of recognizing the need to change, acknowledging the path of change, and recognizing when to change?

Qualification, therefore, becomes a different acronym, referred to as "taking the customer's TEMP." In *The Transparency Sale*, that's T-E-M-P. However, I've recently realized that it may need to be TEMPT, with an added T. Maybe I should refer to it as qualifying whether a prospected is appropriately TEMPTed, as defined by five buyer-centric perspectives on deal qualification:

1. **T**rigger: Does the buyer see that their status quo is no longer sustainable? Do we believe it to be the case?
2. **E**ngagement: An engaged buyer is evidenced in their willingness to put you on their calendar.
3. **M**obilizer: This concept comes from *The Challenger Customer*,[26] but are we attached to someone who is capable of mobilizing change within their organization?
4. **P**lan: An engaged buyer is also willing to chart a path. Are they willing to take a journey with us, and discuss/collaborate on what that journey will look like?
5. **T**ransparency: Are they okay with what we don't do? Have we addressed the elephant in the room? Will the truth sell it?

3) CELEBRATE THE . . . LOSSES

An accurate forecast is only possible through transparent leadership, creating a culture of trust, where both the good and the bad are shared as positives. To acquire and retain even a fighting chance at an accurate forecast begins with creating a transparent culture.

In the most obvious statement I can make, losing deals, losing clients, losing momentum, and even losing deal value comes with the role your team members are living. So, if you know losses are part of the job, is there anyone out there who believes that losing slowly is the best policy?

Nobody has ever said, "I would prefer to work an entire sales cycle before finding out that we've lost . . . versus finding out at the beginning. Working entire losing sales cycles are great learning experiences, and losing builds character!"

Worthington Holman, author of the 1912 book *Ginger Talks*, captured the sentiment of time efficiency so eloquently years ago: "Your time is your capital, your stock in trade. It is the only kind of capital that costs you nothing to get and everything to lose. The successful salesman hoards minutes and hours as a miser hoards gold. The spendthrift of time is a sure candidate for failure."

But we often lose slowly anyway. Why? It starts with you, as the sales leader. Traditional sales leadership approaches to what is measured and enforced disincentivizes sellers from quickly qualifying *out* of opportunities they are likely to lose. A lost deal is one where we were outsold. We prioritize pipeline loads over pipeline quality. We prioritize prospecting skills over qualification skills. Sprinkle in the subconscious internal battle we all develop with the sunk-cost fallacy, which describes when our brains trick us to keep investing in a losing opportunity based on the investment and endorphin rush we've already experienced, and you've got the recipe for wasted effort and a misleading pipeline.

THE PIPELINE COVERAGE MYTH

We must also throw out the concept of the "pipeline-to-quota requirement ratio," which sounds like this, "We close 25–35% of our qualified pipe, so our pipeline needs to be 4 times our quota at all times to ensure we always have enough to hit our targets." This sounds so logical that it was a regular part of my own sales leadership repertoire.

This ratio of pipeline to quota is logical if we're looking at it from a pure algebra perspective, where:

$$\text{(Quarterly Target)} \times \text{(Percentage of Your Qualified Pipeline You Close)} = \text{The Amount of Qualified Pipeline You Need}$$

As sales leaders, growing up in the profession, we have all seen diagrams like this before, the "proper sales funnel."[27]

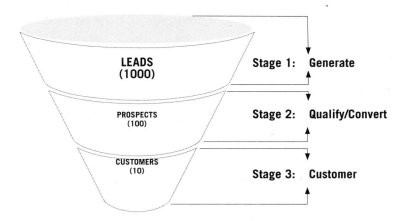

LEADS (1000)	Stage 1:	Generate
PROSPECTS (100)	Stage 2:	Qualify/Convert
CUSTOMERS (10)	Stage 3:	Customer

More leads equals more qualified prospects. More qualified prospects leads to more sales. It's math! We measure the volume at the top of the funnel as a measure of our expected results to come out of the bottom.

I now realize that the math is correct, but not the logic.

My first real sales job was with an overnight shipping company called Airborne Express. Living in Southern California, I thought I was so cool being provided with a company car, a baby-blue Chevy Corsica, which I affectionately referred to as my "Porsche-ica."

Along with that car, I was provided other things that weren't as great: I was also awarded an old-school jackass of a boss, whom we'll call Brandon, because that was his name. Brandon required that we wear a suit and tie every day. I only had enough money for two suits, bought from TJ Max, which I wore down to the threads. The environment he created was *only* about metrics, which he beat us with.

The beatings . . . I mean metrics . . . centered around three sales activity requirements. The first was a requirement to make 60 cold phone outreaches per day. The second requirement was to have a minimum of 20 face-to-face interactions per week. The third was a requirement to have 3 new companies shipping with us per week.

It was all in the numbers. If you were sick that week, it didn't matter. You still had to hit your weekly metrics. When I had a 102 fever and wanted to stay home, he told me how he closed his biggest deal when he had pneumonia and to "get (my) ass into the office if I wanted to keep my job."

Each Friday, our office received a printed-out listing of every shipment from our region for the previous week. A stack of dot matrix continuous paper, lined with small font shipments from hundreds of companies. My territory was 760 square miles, from City of Industry, California, out to Riverside east to west, and Glendora down to Chino north to south. My peer went through it with me, and his territory was just as large. We had to go through and provide our boss with the three new ones that started shipping that week due to our efforts—matched up against our proof that we: (a) called them at some point, and (b) met with them at some point.

Yes, we had to note every call and every meeting. No, you didn't want to leave on Friday afternoon only having proven that your efforts resulted in fewer than three new companies shipping with us that week. Yes, the algebra was correct most of the time:

60 cold outreaches per day yielded 4 new appointments scheduled.

---

4 appointments per day = 20 face-to-face interactions per week.

On average, 20 meetings ≥ 3 new companies shipping with us.

Algebra for algebra's sake ignores the common sense needed behind the metrics. The questions you, as a sales leader, should be asking are:

1. Why did it take 60 cold outreaches to yield 4 new appointments? Could we better identify who we are calling, do a better job preparing for those calls, and only need 30 cold outreaches to achieve the same result?

2. Why did it take 20 meetings to convert 3 companies into shipping with us? Could we be more effective in the meetings we do have, and only need 10 meetings to achieve the same result?

When a sales leader proclaims the pipeline-to-quota requirement as stated at the beginning of this section, where we must all have four times our quota in pipeline, what did you do, as a salesperson? I know what I did. I filled my pipeline with four times my quota to satisfy my manager, but it was filled primarily with crap.

Empower your team not only through enabling them to better prepare and qualify, but also through what you measure. Stop assuming that the ratios are optimal, so pounding the "quantity" drum is the answer. Focus on why those ratios are what they are, not the ratios themselves. Ask yourself, "Why are we only able to close one-fourth of the opportunities we deemed as qualified or worth investing our time in? Could we do a better job of qualifying *in* and *out* opportunities, to where our ratio moves closer to two times needed versus four times?"

Quality over quantity is often said but rarely practiced amongst sales leaders. You have an opportunity to be the leader who leads a team to use their time better, better service their resources, spend less time on the losers, and more time finding, developing, and winning the winners.

The alternative? Managing to averages will make you and your team average.

QUALIFICATION ENABLEMENT

Deal qualification seller development is an oft-overlooked skill but could arguably be one of the most important to maximize the revenue capacity of an individual rep.

Working the right deals, at the right time, with the optimal mutual outcome is what often sets apart the top performers from the middle of the pack. It starts with our messaging. You might be surprised to hear this, but I advocate for leading with transparency. While transparency sells better than perfection, it also qualifies *in* or *out* quickly and firmly.

"Based on our initial understanding of your environment and desired outcomes, there are a couple of areas where we have a bit of concern around our fit. Can we address those first? If those are going to be showstoppers for you, best we both know that up front versus three months down the road, right?"

Or "Given our understanding of your environment, the investment is likely to be between $X and $Y. If that's way off from your expectations, let's address that upfront, so we don't waste your valuable time, either."

It helps the buyer predict their experience faster, with the side effect of a faster sales cycle. It establishes your relationship on a foundation of trust, with the side effect of adding a differentiator in your favor—you differentiate in the way you sell. Regarding setting up the pricing conversation early, if your salespeople are investing time talking about a seven-figure deal with a four-figure buyer, one of them is in the wrong discussion, right?

If there's something off about the fit, the customer will find out . . . either during the cycle or after they've purchased. Either way, it's not good.

Would you rather that information come from you or your competitor?

Would you prefer to control the message or let the competitor deliver the news?

And if it's a showstopper, would you rather know sooner or later?

Would you prefer the prospect drift along like a log on a lazy river, in hopes they realize the river ends with a huge waterfall months into the cycle? Or worse, right *after* they signed on with you?

Work with your marketing department to curate information around your pros and cons. Read customer reviews. Solicit feedback from your customers who renew (ask them why), those customers who buy more, customers who advocate, and especially customers who leave. What are the common themes? Due to the proliferation of reviews and feedback on everything we do, buy, and experience, it's all out there. Curate it, inform your messaging with it, and lead with it!

As I speak with sales leaders and sales enablers, qualification enablement is rarely discussed as a priority. Most discussions center on prospecting and negotiations. The opportunity to lead your team to growth is hiding in your qualification. The second-best thing behind winning is losing quickly. We can foster an environment where losing quickly isn't a punishable offense. The result is an optimized use of our team's time and a more accurate forecast.

THE SUNK-COST FALLACY

The "sunk-cost fallacy (SCF) refers to a greater tendency to continue an endeavor once an investment in time, effort, or money has been made."[28] It's an inherent bias we all have, causing us to ignore the ongoing cost of working on something we have already invested time, resources, and dollars into, even though we know there is unlikely to be a reward for doing so.

Salespeople get a little endorphin hit when they have found an opportunity worth pursuing. There is time invested in finding the opportunity, along with all the positive feelings associated with adding the opportunity to their pipeline. The opportunity is there, like a freshly washed car in a parking lot. You, as the sales leader, see it sitting there. You subconsciously feel better about your potential performance, and maybe even the rep herself. You have all fallen in love with this opportunity without even realizing it.

It dawns on you. This deal is going to be unprofitable for the business or highly likely to be lost to the competitor or the buyer's status quo.

But there's still a chance. So, we keep going. We keep investing that valuable time. Occasionally, it turns out you were right, and you could salvage the opportunity. However, those rare wins of a mismatched opportunity are the exceptions.

Could your time have been spent more wisely prospecting and developing opportunities with a much higher propensity for both short- and long-term benefit? Probably.

Celebrate the losses. Yes. Seriously. While we can flip tradition in the areas described above, empathically celebrating the losses for the effort and the lessons learned reinforces pipeline integrity and forecast accuracy. From this approach, you will quickly hone your team's focus, better identifying the warning signs earlier in the rest of your prospecting efforts and existing pipeline. Your pipeline will cease to be filled with crap. Would you rather have a pipeline which only represents two times your team's quota but is made up entirely of highly qualified opportunities, or a pipeline representing four times your team's quota, much of which is likely garbage? Your rep is already getting punished in their wallet. Jacklyn just lost a big deal she worked six months to develop? Do a champagne toast to her! Give her the opportunity to relish in her effort and ask with no tone of ever casting blame, "If we were to start this opportunity all over again, what would we have done differently? What do we know now that we wish we knew then?" Raise their morale and engagement, create over-the-top learning experiences from the losses, and see your team's transparency with their pipeline blossom.

4) MAKING *COMMIT* A DIRTY WORD

"What's your commit?" asks your sales leader. Often in front of a room full of your peers.

How do you respond? You begin to think . . .

- "Thankfully, I have a really full pipeline. But I'm not about to commit to 200%. Especially in front of a room full of my peers. I'll under- commit and overdeliver." In other words, I'll lie. Why sign up for a big number?

or

- "My pipeline is pretty weak this quarter. But I'm not about to commit 50%. I mean, my boss and her boss are both in the room. I'll just commit my quota." In other words, I'll lie. I'll avoid the short-term punishment of committing under my target and push off the punishment until I miss the target in three months.

Then, a thought hits you. "I can't just say my quota. That'll be viewed as just doing the minimum. I'll say 105%." In other words, I'll lie.

Now that the death march around the room is over, where every quota-bearing rep has had an opportunity to lie, an interesting dynamic occurs. Somehow every single rep has just committed to hitting their quarterly quota. How often does every single salesperson on your team hit? It's rare enough that you always remember when it occurs. In this commit environment, the expectation is set every single quarter.

The sales leader then adds up the commits. You're signed up—in front of your peers.

As the months pass and the quarter ends, regardless of how the team performed, individual forecast accuracy is atrocious.

What is the purpose of the commit? In my engagements with leaders who swear by them, the three most common answers I hear have been:

1. "I use it to create my forecast." Oh, good idea. A forecast built on a foundation of lies. (Sorry.)
2. "I have to forecast my business to my boss and our board. I want the reps to have an opportunity to do the same in front of their peers." There's a difference between a *forecast* and a *commit*. What you just had the reps do was publicly pledge to something they probably don't believe and certainly can't completely control.

3. "The reps need to be accountable." They already are . . . to themselves, their quota, their paycheck, their careers, their team, and if they like who they work for, the organization.

Let's think about it. When a customer says *yes*, guess what? The odds of that deal closing are still not 100%. They're likely closer to 75%. Three out of four will close, but one out of four won't. There will be a failure to come to terms. That buyer did not realize the additional steps required to finalize the purchase internally. There are a multitude of reasons why this opportunity could go south.

A customer has said *yes* and has now gone through a round of contract redlines. The odds are now around 90% of the deal closing. One out of 10 deals where everything is buttoned up will still not close. A company will get acquired. A reorganization will happen, a board member will force their hand toward a competitor, or countless other things (that have all happened to my teams and me at some point in my career).

I have never once uttered the word *commit* in a request.

Why?

Well, first, I've never been asked to give a *commit* to my CEO or my board. I've been asked to give a *forecast*. I feel that I'm not being a strong leader by asking my team to do something I wouldn't do.

Second, our wiring as human beings drives an avoidance of short-term pain over the avoidance of long-term pain. We'll lie now to avoid a short-term pain (or receive a short-term reward) and will concern ourselves with the long-term consequences later. In other words, the brain is wired to make things up in those environments.

And the biggest reason? Associating the word *commit* creates anxiety that results in lost deal amnesia, or more broadly, "lost deal transparency."

What does lost deal transparency mean?

First, let's imagine that the deal that has been committed falls apart. As a sales leader, you want to create an environment where your sellers come to you first for support. However, in a commit environment, you as the sales leader are the *last* person they turn to for guidance.

Instead, your salesperson is now spending the next few hours deciding what to do . . . by themselves. Telling the manager is the last thing they're about to do—because the phrase, "It sounds like we're getting outsold" is sure to follow.

Focus 1 for the rep is "How do I save this?" and focus 2 is "How do I present this to my manager to make sure he/she does not assign fault to me?" Now there's a lack of visibility to the leader who may be able to help. The story the leader receives may not be entirely true. The rep may dig a deeper hole. And due to the story you as a leader receive, you may help dig that deeper hole. All is lost . . . including your forecast.

Transparency isn't just something that works when working with prospects and customers. It's even more magical within the four walls of your organization.

So, instead of commits, why not spend the time coaching them, honing the fine art and science of owning their territory forecast, like you, their leader?

Forecasting in business should be like forecasting the weather. Nobody is expecting perfection. But everyone is expecting you to be within a standard deviation of your forecast or so.

In other words, if you're planning a backyard barbecue in a week, you need to plan. You'll need to buy the food and drinks, set up the space, and invite your friends. If the 10-day forecast says it's going to be 70°F and sunny, it's a go. When barbecue day comes and it's 67°F and sunny, all is good. Not a perfect forecast, but close enough to plan and resource.

However, if barbecue day comes and it's 40°F and raining sideways, there's a big problem. If barbecue day comes and it's 98°F and humid, that's equally a big problem.

The goal of sales forecasting is to be in range. Teaching reps that wildly under- or overachieving a forecast is not good. Reward forecast accuracy and coach coach coach!

The fruits of having your team's honesty and transparency regarding their potential performance exponentially outweigh any value from a commit session.

If the news is bad, where the rep is forecasting to be under their target, encourage that transparency! It's an opportunity to help. To support. To coach. When stuff happens, creating a transparent sales environment will have the rep coming to you first and immediately for help instead of a lecture.

And, for goodness' sake, have these conversations privately! I still get anxiety just recalling the times I've been involved in a public commit death march.

Foster a culture where people aren't afraid to make mistakes. Foster a culture where there's accountability coupled with honesty. A good first step is to remove the word *commit* and its associated message from your leadership philosophy.

Transparency wins!

5) RETHINKING TRADITIONAL KEY PERFORMANCE INDICATORS

I get it. We've been brought up in selling environments where we were shoulder to shoulder. It was easy to see who was working and who wasn't. However, in a remote setting, or even a hybrid environment (which I would surmise will be the way forward for years to come), poor sales leadership in terms of measures will be the demise of culture and the poison that shrinks tenures.

What do we measure?

In a scene from the 1980's classic comedy movie *Caddyshack*, Judge Smails (played by Ted Knight) speaks to fellow member Ty Webb (played by Chevy Chase) about his golf game.

Judge Smails: "Ty, what did you shoot today?"

Ty Webb: "Oh, Judge, I don't keep score."

Judge Smails: "Then how do you measure yourself with other golfers?"

Ty Webb: "By height."

By height. Clearly a sarcastic answer, but when looking at the multitude of metrics that can be measured to assess anything in sales, how do we know which metrics provide an indication of anything that could be deemed useful or predictable?

Transparent sales leadership provides team members a lens into how you think about the business. If that lens opens up a world where those running behind you think you are so scattered that it erodes their confidence in you, that's a problem, right?

If you are measuring everything, are you measuring anything that matters? By gaining a focus on the metrics that truly drive results, then sharing those metrics, you: (a) focus, and (b) build confidence in those around you.

In *The Transparency Sale*, I took on this topic from an individual contributor's perspective. However, the metrics are the same from the lens of sales leadership. Four primary numbers contribute to results. Yes, just four. While we could measure 100 plus, a focus on just four of them will hone your focus and make you look smart in the process.

The results of your sales organization are a combination of:

1. Number of opportunities your team has to work on (O)
2. The dollar value of each of those opportunities ($)
3. What percentage of those opportunities you win (%)
4. How long it takes for you to win the opportunities you win (CL)

These four core metrics are volume, size, win rate, and time. That's all. Now, let's talk about how we use these four to drive proactive visibility into performance and inform a more accurate forecast.

THE SALES LEADER'S USAGE: COMMUNICATION AND TRANSPARENCY

Years ago, while attending a keynote by author and marketing expert Seth Godin, he asked the audience to do something. It was a room filled with hundreds of people, and the activity asked was simple.

"I want everyone in this room to raise their right hand just as high as they can raise it."

Looking around the room, he had almost complete compliance.

"Is that as high as you can do it?"

After a moment of taking in the audience, he then added, "Now, I want you to raise it a little higher."

Like magic, every hand in the room went up just a little bit higher.

This idea has stuck with me ever since. As a sales leader at the time, I was asking my team to raise their right hand every day, every week, every month, and every year just as high as they could. Then, once the calendar year flipped to January 1, I asked them to raise it a little higher. As the communicator of such an ask, we probably don't give it another thought.

"We have to grow. You must do more. Period."

But as the recipient of such an ask, it sounds ridiculous. "Do you, sales leader, not think I'm already raising my hand as high as it will go every single day?"

And as the leader, you think, "Well, you just proved to me that you weren't raising it as high as it'll go. There's always more."

Well, you can both be right. We can recognize that asking for an endless amount of "more" loses its effectiveness. However, we can also acknowledge that the framing of such a request, sprinkled in with a little math, can make all the difference in inspiration to achieve.

Every year, your organization has a growth goal that trickles down to the sales team in the form of higher quotas. I, as a sales leader, never enjoyed delivering the news that "your quotas are 20% higher this year than they were last year." As a salesperson, you just did everything you could to achieve the highest outcome possible, and now you're telling me to do 20% more? Are you crazy?

With the logic of the hand raise, yes. However, the path to 20% is much simpler to envision if we just do some simple math. As a salesperson and as a sales team, if you can drive tiny incremental improvements in each of the four categories of KPIs, the result is considerable. The way the math works out, if each rep does the following, their results will grow by 22%:

1. Grow "O" (the number of qualified opportunities) by 5%. For example, if you work 20 qualified opportunities in a year, 5% is just 1 more opportunity.

2. Grow "$" (the dollar value of each opportunity) by 5%. For example, if your average deal size is $40,000, 5% is just $2,000 more per opportunity.

3. Grow "%" (your win rate, the percentage of qualified opportunities you win over the total) by 5%. For example, if you currently win 60% of your qualified opportunities, 5% is just a 3% improvement, which could be one or two deals.

4. Shrink "CL" (your sales cycle length from qualification to close) by 5%. For example, if your current sales cycles average 50 days, that's finding a way to remove 2 1/2 days from qualification to close.

If you're not getting better, you're getting worse. Small tweaks and small improvements lead to big results. The math always works—5% improvement equals 22% greater results. Delivering the news of a 20% higher quota becomes simple when viewed through a lens of, "What does 5% really mean?" It means tiny improvements across four categories. That's all.

THE MATH

Do you want to sound smart to your team, your peers in leadership, your board, your investors, or anyone else who will listen (i.e., the next position you interview for)? This little focus on how you think about metrics is a great place to start. Oh, and there's a reason it will make you sound smart; it will make you smart to proactively see what's going on in your business. It will force you to think beyond the silos of traditional metrics and save you a ton of time wasted looking at metrics with very little meaning.

Here's what I did:

1. Make sure you have developed a consistent definition for what constitutes an opportunity (O). Each month, on a spreadsheet, list out how many opportunities your team has developed that month. Count them up.

2. Do the same for your ClosedWon new business ($), calculating their average deal size. To make the math work, if you experience anomalies, you may want to consider using a median instead of a mean not to skew your data.

3. Do the same for your win rate (%), determining what constitutes a win and a loss. It doesn't have to be perfect, just consistent.

4. Establish a rule for when an opportunity actively enters the sales cycle, and in combination with 3 above, you should be able to begin to get consistency around your cycle lengths (CL).

Next, on the spreadsheet, begin to measure the improvement or decline month over month, quarter over quarter, and year over year.

Explain to those constituents who matter the results formula, then show the data. For example: "This past quarter, we experienced a decline in the number of qualified opportunities (O) of 2%, however, were able to achieve our targets because we experienced a 7% increase in deal values ($), a 10% increase in our win rate (%), and we shrunk cycle lengths (CL) by 6%. We're working with our internal teams to determine the cause of the reduction in qualified opportunities. However, it may turn out to be a good thing. Initial indications tell us that we did a better job of qualification, which led to the increases in the other categories. We may want to point our organization more aggressively in that better focused direction."

THE SALES LEADER'S USAGE: COACHING

Take two salespeople from my past, Rob and Dana.

Rob was an opportunity generation machine. His O (number of opportunities) was always the highest in the organization.

Dana, on the other hand, was not an opportunity generation machine. Her O was typically in the lower half of the team.

As a sales leader of that team, you might want to parade Rob around the office as the top-performing hero, and you may be considering putting Dana on a performance improvement plan. However, when investigating the results formula, your perspective quickly shifts.

You see, out of the two, Dana was the top performer. She worked a smaller number of opportunities (O), but each was a higher dollar value ($), while her win rate (%) and cycle lengths (CL) were incredibly efficient. Dana consistently crushed Rob because Rob's deals tended to stretch out, and his losses to the status quo were frequent.

From a coaching perspective, what do you do?

While you likely do not want to ignore the issue of Dana's opportunity volume, as a sales leader, you must look beyond the silos of the individual metrics and instead investigate the ratios. Then, use those ratios in your determinations and coaching. As a top performer, Dana could be an incredible resource to the rest of the team in her focus, her deal qualification, and how she executes the process. Rob could be an asset in finding and developing new opportunities. Rob's lessons could be valuable to Dana in helping her improve her O and experience even more incredible results. With Rob, we spent time with him finding the right opportunities and eventually moved him into a team lead role for our sales development organization and out of the full-cycle account executive role. He flourished.

If we look at numbers in a silo, we would have made the wrong decisions, ones that were likely to drive Rob and Dana to disengagement, lower performance, and potentially even turnover.

Rob and Dana's manager was a master of this approach, taking it a step further—to the ultimate level of transparency. Each month, he shared a spreadsheet with the four KPIs of the previous month listed for each rep. Each reps' name was kept anonymous, represented by a letter (A, B, C, . . .). The rest of the team would look at the spreadsheet, then select who they believed the rep of the month should be by voting on the accompanying letter. The winner would be selected based on all four metrics, not just one.

This approach served a higher purpose. The sales leader ensured that every person on his team knew what was expected and what was being measured. No secrets. Higher engagement.

PUTTING IT ALL TOGETHER: THE FORECAST

Want to know how we created a forecast with incredible 90-day visibility and accuracy? Here goes . . .

Step 1: Tight forecast accuracy, which does not rely on luck, starts with your sales forecasting culture, as described above. Without the environment created, supported, and reinforced by every leader in your organization, as the old saying goes, even a blind squirrel finds a nut once in a while, but it's no way to live.

Step 2: Get tactical. You can use this chart below as a starting point, which we will go through in detail to help you either get started or adjust your current approach.

The chart details the stages we used to guide the investigation, classification, reality, and forecast of our deals. It did not matter whether we talked about a large, six-figure-plus transaction or a faster, four-figure opportunity. We discussed each opportunity through the lens of the buyer journey.

Across the top, you'll see the buyer journey defined as "Why change?", "Why us?", then "Why now?" These become the baseline for discussion around the opportunities themselves.

FORECASTING: BUYER & SELLER BEHAVIOR / ALIGNMENT

Sales Melon

	WHY CHANGE?		WHY US?		WHY NOW?		
	Suspect 0%	Discover 10%	Confirm 25%	Decide 50%	Selected 75%	Negotiate 90%	Closed Won 100%
THEM	Customer Is "Engaged"	Alignment Conceptually Understood	Mutual Learning Engagement	We're a Finalist (1 of 2 or 3) Pending Yes or No	Verbally Selected Ready for Agreement	No Deal Breakers Signature Near	Agreement Executed
US	Teach Provide Personalized Value	Trigger Engaged Mobilizer Plan Transparency	Tailored Alignment on Pros & Cons of Our Solution	No Surprises Right: - Solution - Power - Dollars - Timing	Agreement Sent Mutually Agreed Plan	Finalizing T's & C's	Confirmation Value Realization
	___ Days / Weeks	___ Days / Weeks	___ Days / Weeks	___ Days / Weeks	___ Days / Weeks	___ Days / Weeks	

QUALIFIED PIPELINE

Under each buyer behavior stage are the individual stages you and the buyer are going through together. In each column, there are two categories of activities:

Them: If you were to ask the prospect/buyer what they are doing, thinking, or believe is coming next, what would be their answer? Their answer might be different depending on where they are along the buying journey. This row aligned under each forecast stage column can be your guide.

Us: Based on where the buyer is along their journey, this row describes the activities the seller should consider or be focused on to confirm where the buyer is in their journey.

You'll notice an arrow that stretches from the beginning (left side) of the 10% column through to the ending (right side) of the 90% column containing the words "Qualified Pipeline." When an opportunity is in one of these stages, it represents the opportunities that can be forecasted.

Step 3: Understand the stages and ensure each of your team members understand them well, too.

- Suspect (0%): These are the organizations and opportunities where the prospect appears, from the outside, to meet the criteria of what would constitute a good potential client for your organization. Evidence is typically found in whether your organization has marketed to this client—as long as your marketing organization is well focused. What is the buyer doing in this stage? They have committed to putting time to engage with you on their calendar. Evidence of engagement is shown in a prospect's willingness to contribute their own time, documented, and allocated in their own calendar. This stage is prequalified, in that the company appears to have a heartbeat, and engagement and assessment is required before moving into a qualified stage.
- Discover (10%): In this stage, the prospect understands your value proposition and continues to be engaged. Your seller is now engaged in exploring whether there is a trigger by which their status quo is worth changing, whether this individual or individuals are capable of mobilizing change in

their organization, whether they are willing to chart a plan or path to coming to a mutual decision together with you and your organization, and *confidence that the truth will sell it.*

- Confirm (25%): This is where mutual learning occurs. The prospect has communicated the reality that doing something different tomorrow than they are doing today is necessary and desired. They are as engaged in predicting what their experience will be with you as you are with them. They are likely doing the same with other options, competitors, pieces of solutions, or even potentially addressing the issue on their own. Your organization's focus should continue to be expectation setting, transparently partnering with the prospect to help them determine the pros of your solution, the cons of your solution, the potential pros and cons of their other options, and painting a clear picture of the journey to fully realized change.

- Decide (50%): You have reached the decision phase when the mutual learning is all but completed. Your prospect is deciding, and that decision should be focused on, at most, one or two alternatives. The prospect should be able to articulate your pros and cons, your solution as it relates to their specific environment, the required investment, and their own path to formalizing the relationship and moving forward together.

- Selected (75%): The prospect has communicated that you are the selected solution for change within the prospect's organization. They should also now be focused on ironing out the details, formalizing the relationship. As the selling organization, your focus becomes the same, aligning with the prospect on the plan, along with ensuring resource alignment in preparation for fulfilling the agreement.

- Negotiation (90%): Once the agreement process has begun and the prospect's organization sees no deal breakers, where we are down to the small details and waiting for signature, it now belongs in the negotiation stage.

- ClosedWon (100%): The relationship is now formalized, typically in the form of a mutually signed agreement. It is time to execute. But first, ensure that any expectations set are met immediately. There is nothing worse than a prospect signing an agreement, allocating their own precious budget to a project, embracing change, taking on the risk associated with the unknown, then not hearing a peep from the vendor for hours, days, even weeks after signature. Reinforce their endorphin rush from finalizing the agreement while those endorphins are fresh.

Step 4: Under each stage, you will also find "___ Days/Weeks." Ask yourself the question, how long, on average, should an opportunity stay in this stage? Then, determine how long before an opportunity sits in that stage before you should truly question whether it belongs there. For example, a prospect indicated that they have completed their evaluation and are making a final decision between you and a competitor. That opportunity resides in the "Decide" stage, correct? Now, ask yourself this question: "If an opportunity sat in this stage for six months, would that be a concern?" Your answer would likely be "Of course!" Then keep lowering the time. How about three months? One month? Two weeks? You'll hit a point where you will think, "___ weeks is ok, given we still have engagement with the prospect, but anything longer would be concerning." Put that number in the blank. Do the same with each stage. You may have different timeframes for different-sized transactions, where a large transaction may be months associated with each stage, whereas a small transaction may be in hours. Moving forward, this will be an evaluation point with your reps in determining whether an opportunity is in the correct stage, and an early warning signal as well.

Step 5: If you've set up the environment well, where forecast accuracy and even losses are celebrated, managers work with their reps the first of the month to validate the accuracy of the dollar amounts, stages, and stage durations as described in Step 4. For each opportunity set to close in the 90 days that make up your quarter, add up the dollar amount in each stage, then multiply by the stage %.

For example, if you have $250,000 in the "Confirm" (25%) stage, you'll multiply $250,000 by .25. That total of $62,500 will be the number represented in your forecast. Total up each calculated amount by stage, and you'll have an overall total for the upcoming 90-day period.

Step 6: Snapshot the amount. Once you've been doing this for 90-days, you'll want to compare the total to the actual and see how close you've gotten. If you're far off the first time, investigate the why. Look at the deals and determine whether there were lessons to be learned by how deals were calculated, how you, your reps, or your managers (if you manage managers) staged and totaled the pipeline. Is your environment not supporting accuracy just yet? Evaluate and adjust.

Step 7: The simple task of totaling each stage, then multiplying the result by the stage % will never be the end-all accurate result. Over time, you'll notice that deals in "Decide" don't perfectly close 50% of the time. It may be 54% of the time, or even higher. As mentioned in Step 6, snapshot each 90-day rollup and compare it to your 90-day actuals. Over time, you'll see a trend. Here's the amazing part! We found that our rollup was, on average, 82% accurate over each 90-day period. One 90-day period was 79% accurate. The next was 85%. The next was 83%. The next? 80%.

Figure out how close the rollup is, on average. We'd use an average of our last four 90-day periods. This became our forecast multiplier, which accounted for the fact that each stage percentage couldn't possibly be exactly as described (10%, 25%, 50%, etc.). And, if you have deals that appear and close within 90 days, and potentially don't show up at the beginning of a quarter, the multiplier accounts for those, too . . . assuming you have a consistent level of fast close deals over each 90-day period.

Step 8: Generate the forecast. It's a calculation of: (a) each deal in each stage's anticipated deal value multiplied by the stage %, then (b) multiplying that total by the multiplier determined in Step 7. That amount is your 90-day forecast.

Buyer-behavior focused versus seller-activity focused will always win in your sales forecasting. Coupling that with the environment you create around forecast accuracy, and you have the recipe for a more accurate forecast.

Accurate forecasting is possible. It begins with how you create a culture that embraces transparency.

CHAPTER 7

FOCUS
FIELD
FUNDAMENTALS
FORECAST
FUN

*Work, and work hard, at your business, but do not let that be
the only end to your life. The golden calf is only plated. And
when old age comes, you will not be a dried-up bag of money.*

— Nathaniel Clark Fowler, Jr., *Practical Salesmanship*, 1911

F INALLY, AND POTENTIALLY MOST IMPORTANTLY, TO CREATE A MAGNETIC, engaged workplace, we must create an environment where your team has fun every day, loving what they do, who they do it with, and who they do it for.

The oft-used word is *engagement*. Engagement comes from you, the leader, and is the key to performance, the mental health of both yourself and your team, predictability, reduced turnover, and even speed to hire.

"Engagement is a kind of psychological presence" while performing a job.[29] We're emotionally, cognitively, and physically attached to it. We're motivated to engage in the work and develop meaningful relationships with co-workers up and down. Work is no longer a nine-to-five job. It's something we consider and think about on and off all day and every day. The fun factor correlates directly with your state of mind.

When my intrinsic inspiration suffered in my own career, my state of mind suffered along with it. Those around me could see it. I brought it home with me every day to my family. It had everything to do with my immediate manager. It had nothing to do with my pay.

INTRINSIC INSPIRATION

True or false? "Sales reps are coin-operated."

The answer is *true* when you're doing *it* wrong as a sales leader.

What is *it*? *It* is sales leadership. *It* is the prioritization of your leadership approach and style. What gets an individual out of bed in the morning? What drives them to achieve each day? If you have created an environment for your sales team where the only motivation they have each day is through the promise of dollars, you have missed out on an incredible opportunity to maximize your team's performance. You have missed out on an incredible opportunity to lengthen the tenure of the individuals on your team. You have missed out on an incredible opportunity to speed the time it takes to hire additional team members because your current team members are screaming from the mountaintops their passion for their work.

Why are you still reading this book? I'm guessing nobody is paying you to read this. There's no quiz at the end. You are reading this book driven primarily by your intrinsic inspiration.

Intrinsic inspiration is your actions being driven without any tangible reward for doing so. You are engaging in behavior driven by something inside of you, versus an external motivation provided outside of you.

For example, a behavior that requires an extrinsic or "coin-operated" motivation is one that is not exciting, challenging, requires little creativity, complexity, or even brainpower.

George: "Hey, thanks for coming over. Could you go into my backyard and dig some holes for some new bushes I'm having put in?"

You: "Ummm, no. That sounds awful."

George: "I'll pay you $100 per hole."

You: "Where's the shovel?"

In this instance, you had to be *extrinsically* motivated, which is necessary when we don't find intrinsic motivation from doing the job.

In an optimal selling environment, variable compensation's role is as a positive, secondary reinforcement—in other words, a *reward* for successful outcomes in performing the work versus the *motivator*.

It's positive, in that it's a reward for desired behavior (versus a punishment for bad behavior), and it's secondary in that it's meant to condition paired reinforcement.

Yes, variable compensation is essential, but only a portion of what drives an individual. The key to having reps who show up every day, do their best, stay, and tell their friends is in creating an environment where they are rewarded for doing work they are intrinsically motivated to do.

And engaged employees consistently outperform, have longer tenures, and are more likely to assist in recruiting than disengaged employees, according to Captain Obvious.

Intrinsic inspiration? Those are the motivations brought forth from within an individual—within yourself.

Extrinsic motivation? Those are motivations that come from outside of an individual—like money or trophies.

Where does that intrinsic inspiration come from?

It's time to talk about our feelings.

"In a sales leadership book? Ugh, that sounds gross. I'm putting this book down!"

Well, the good news is, with the framework described here in Part 1 of this book internalized, once put into action, you have moved appreciably above the average sales leader. You have a structure and process from which you can plan, strategize, consistently execute, and communicate to everyone that runs behind you and everyone you run behind.

There's an opportunity to extend your lead. Through a firm understanding of the feelings that drive us as human beings and specifically your sales team to maximum performance, we can create optimized revenue-generating environments. Imagine seeing these results while also having every participant in it having fun on that journey together.

Well, we're not talking about love or hate in these feelings. We are referring to the six drivers of *intrinsic inspiration*.

The most significant results come from the most outstanding teams who are surrounded by the greatest cultures. The importance of optimizing the fun in your team cannot be understated and is the focus of Part 2, "The Behavioral Science of Intrinsic Inspiration."

PART TWO

THE BEHAVIORAL SCIENCE OF INTRINSIC INSPIRATION

I believe in today and the work I am doing, in tomorrow and the work I hope to do and in the sure reward which the future holds.

— Edwin Osgood Grover, *The Salesman's Creed*, 1905

ACKSON HAS A CHRONIC HEALTH CONDITION; IT'S POTENTIALLY deadly if not managed correctly. His doctor has prescribed a specific course of action, including medications, alterations to his diet, and ongoing therapy. According to the Centers for Disease Control and Prevention, 60% of Americans have at least one chronic disease, and 40% have two or more. There's a better than 50/50 chance that you are like Jackson.[30]

Medications and short-term therapies are easy, right? Well, as it turns out, 20% to 30% of short-term therapies prescribed by their doctors are ignored, and 20% to 30% of prescriptions prescribed by a medical provider are never filled.[31] A full-on 70% to 80% of lifestyle change recommendations are ignored.[32]

Are all these people who do not follow the advice of doctors in the maintenance of their health stupid? Sure, some may be playing the game of life with less than a full deck of cards. Could there be another reason why individuals are not intrinsically inspired to follow their doctor's advice? Absolutely.

As a sales leader, you are not of the ilk of a doctor to your salespeople. Your team is (hopefully) not suffering from a health-altering condition. If such a large percentage of people don't follow a doctor's advice for health conditions, do you think your team's compliance with your recommendations as a sales leader and guidance will be better or worse?

As neuroscientist Antonio Damasio explains in his book *Descartes' Error*, "We are not thinking machines. We are feeling machines that think."[33] Feelings drive our decisions—to make purchases, prioritize, and make decisions, but in the day-to-day context, to engage.

In their nebulous context, feelings can seem like we're talking about love, hate, anger, and fear. When used as a part of your sales leadership framework for considering, monitoring, and driving intrinsic inspiration, they become a powerful tool for performance, stability, joy, and success.

There are six primary categories of feelings that drive us intrinsically. I had a version of the six we will dig into in detail below and throughout the following few chapters written on a note attached to my computer monitor in my office. It served as a reminder for me during my interactions with my team, peers, and even customers. One of our long-term customers decided not to renew their relationship with our organization. His verbalized reasons were logical, citing a lack of ROI (return on investment). Feelings drove his suppressed reasons. Through transparency, we quickly uncovered those feelings that drove the decision—a lack of partnership.

The same framework served a similar purpose with personnel decisions, discussions around an individual resigning, coaching conversations regarding performance, and even periodic reviews. While I'm biased in my opinion, this framework will change the way you listen, but more importantly, it will change the way you consider culture development and decision-making.

The teams we build have a choice. Every day when they wake up in the morning, are they going to bring their all? Will they follow *your* recommendations? Are they going to stay? Are they going to want to advocate on our behalf, to aid in minimizing turnover and speeding time to hire? That's on you, the sales leader.

You as an individual and those on your team are subconsciously engaged by these six categories of feelings that, when maximized, result in low voluntary turnover and maximized team revenue potential. Balance these six. Use them as a guide to monitor and discuss the engagement of your teams. See the holes before they form.

In the following chapters, we will dig into each one individually. At their highest level, those six you should be providing. They happen to spell out the word *praise*:

1. **Predictability**: We do our best work when we can predict the future. When we go to bed at night, we sleep best and perform best the next day when we know what we'll be waking up to on the next day. Are you consistent as a leader? Does the team know where you are all headed? Does each rep know what their day, week, month, and year might look like? Consistency and expectation drive engagement, unlike the inconsistent, moody, cards-hidden sales leader.

2. **Recognition**: We do our best work when we are recognized for our efforts, validated for the impact, given status in front of others, and provided regular feedback. As a sales leader, establishing regular opportunities to recognize, validate, and give status win out over the old-school "you're lucky you have a job" sales leader.

3. **Aim**: Do your reps know what their work means to you? Do your reps know what their work means to your customers? Do your reps know what their work means to your customers' customers? Working for a purpose—what your company does matters, make sure your reps know it—versus the "you're a number with a number" sales leader.

4. **Independence**: We do our best work when we have autonomy, trust, resources, and independence. Give your team the resources, independence, and control they need to execute their positions independently.

5. **Security**: We do our best work when we are a part of a team. Packs outperform individuals. It is your role as a leader to foster the team, foster security, and ensure each individual feels like someone has their back—versus the disconnected, you-against-everyone-else sales leader.

6. **Equitability**: We do our best work when we feel like "the juice is worth the squeeze." Are the rewards I receive equitable to the output? Are the rewards I receive equitable with others in the same positions? That's not just money. It's the rewards associated with all six categories combined.

When the supply of talent is so much lower than the demand, creating magnetic cultures where people want to come, stay, and tell their friends, focusing on all six versus just compensation and discipline is the way.

Variable compensation wins when it's the REWARD, not the MOTIVATOR.

CHAPTER 8

PREDICTABILITY

You have heard the expression, "I don't know where I'm going, but I'm on my way." That is how the average man enters the profession of selling.

— Norval A. Hawkins, *The Selling Process*, 1920

T'S A HOT DAY. YOUR MOUTH IS DRY, YOU'RE SWEATING, AND SUDDENLY you realize you are thirsty. You grab a glass of water and drink it down. You are no longer feeling thirsty.

In your body, when you drink water, it heads down to your stomach, then off to your large intestine, and eventually reaches your bloodstream. On an empty stomach, that process takes around five minutes. It could take as long as 45 minutes to 2 hours on a full stomach.[34]

So why, when drinking water, do you immediately feel your thirst quenched?

It's because our brains are prediction machines.

Every moment of every day, our brains are taking in the information it receives through the rest of our body's systems, matching it up against what it knows and making bold predictions. Our body matches our dry mouth with the warmth we feel throughout and knows that the combination of the two is a warning signal that we will need hydration, so it brings a feeling of thirst to your consciousness.

The cool water entering your mouth and down your esophagus matches up those feelings to bring to your conscious a resolution to that feeling of thirst, in that help is on the way.

You're walking in a dark forest and hear branches cracking up ahead. Your brain predicts the worst, telling your body, "I don't know what it is, but I'm going to prepare like it's an ax murderer or a bear." Your heart starts racing before you've consciously processed the situation. It's taking in more information, searching for certainty. It may just be the wind, or a squirrel traveling tree to tree. But our brains prepare and rush to prepare for a worst-case scenario first.

We, as human beings, do our best work when we're able to predict. We get our best sleep when we know what we'll be waking up to the next morning. When we do wake up in the morning, our personal engagement is at its peak when we are able to predict our day.

When we are in an uncertain environment, it is taxing on the brain. Our IQ goes down, as our energy-burning brains seek to make sense of the information it is taking in. Think back to March of 2020, when the Covid pandemic hit. We were all sent home. Buyers reprioritized their spending to seek their certain ground. Sales leaders all had to adjust, spending all their time balancing their own need for certainty with creating an environment where their teams could maintain their engagement and productivity. And all the while, many of us were shifting in our personal lives, waiting in line to hoard toilet paper for biological certainty, setting up home offices, and figuring out how to balance our emotional uncertainty with our professional environment.

Human beings are driven to situations or environments where there is a predictable expectation. Individuals tend to be less productive when they have feelings of uncertainty, inconsistency, and instability.

Imagine you walk into the office, and you see your boss walking toward you. She has her head down, doesn't make eye contact, and doesn't acknowledge you. Your brain goes into uncertainty mode. "Wow, she's mad at me about something! I must have done something wrong. I'm in trouble." Maybe she just has something on her mind. Just like our brains preparing for a bear in the forest, our brains are wired to think the worst.

Consistent leadership does not have to mean being consistently warm, consistently gracious, or consistently engaging. Being consistently grumpy and distant is better than being inconsistent. For example, a few years ago, I was running a team at a large technology company. We had been acquired a few months earlier. It was the beginning of a new year, and decisions were being made around organizing the go-to-market. My manager was a sharp, cerebral, but consistently distant person. I could always count on him to bring me down. As an example of bringing me down, once, I was a key contributor on a conference call with several senior leaders, some from the acquiring company, and some from ours. Following an update I provided to the group, one of the European leaders from the acquiring company showered me with praise regarding how the overall onboarding felt like the only truly under-control element of the integration process. I replied to the praise with a thank-you. Moments later, I looked down at my instant messages, and there was a message from my manager, saying, "Don't just take that. Always ask the question around what you could have done better." I replied, "Did you just critique the way I took a compliment?"

I digress. It was the first week of January, and the phone rang. It was that manager. The conversation started with small talk. "How did you celebrate New Year's?" He followed that up with, "How many kids do you have?" "What are their names?" While his interest in my personal life was nice, it was oddly inconsistent with his normal managerial behavior. In all the time I had reported to him, we never once talked about our personal lives. It triggered my subconscious to scream, "What hell is he about to unleash on me?"

Sure enough, hell was unleashed. The post-acquisition reorganization would not be treating me fairly.

You can probably remember a situation where your manager put a meeting on your calendar; an unexpected one-on-one. Your brain probably started spinning. "I wonder what this is about." "Did I do something?" You then message a peer, your friend, spouse, partner, telling them, "I think I may be getting fired."

You are in the office and notice a meeting taking place where your peers are participating in the conference room, and you weren't invited. Your brain punches you with, "Wow, they must not value my opinion." Maybe they're planning your birthday party. Maybe those individuals are getting reprimanded for not being as awesome as you. Again, it's our brain's protection mechanism, instantly thinking the worst.

As a leader, are you consistent? Are you predictable, personally? Your team's ability to predict what you will bring each day is a key component of their intrinsic inspiration—even if you are consistently a jerk.

Are we inadvertently creating uncertainty for our teams? Are we forcing the individuals on our teams to spend unnecessary time and energy seeking predictable ground?

INITIAL EXPECTATIONS

You are setting the prediction in the minds of your team from your first interaction. Often, that first interaction is happening during the interviewing process.

In a sellers' market, where the demand for great salespeople far exceeds the supply, you probably can't help yourself from painting a picture of the role the salesperson is interviewing as being five stars. Even worse, the false expectation setting takes the form of almost presenting the role as being six stars (on a five-star scale). You may be thinking you have to sell the role aggressively to a candidate you perceive as ideal. The downstream damage from overselling and overpromising—then underdelivering has massive repercussions.

There are at least five ways sales leaders tend to overpromise during the first interaction—where the prediction is being created.

THE "CAREER-LADDER" (OVER) PROMISE

This one sounds like: "You'll come in here, crush it, and in 6–12 months, based on our growth projections, you'll have opportunities to get into leadership!"

Often, this overpromise starts with a question you, as the interviewer, ask regarding the candidate's career aspirations.

"Where do you want to be in five years?"

"Well, I eventually want to run a sales team."

"That's great! You've come to the right place!" The next and the next sentence is the "Career Ladder" (Over) Promise. The candidate gets excited about that possibility and takes the position. Later that day, the candidate tells their friends about the new job they'll be starting in a few weeks. "And, I'm going to have an opportunity to run a team within the next 6–12 months!"

The candidate begins and realizes that the same has been said to the other salespeople on your team. There are no more discussions about this career progression. Disengagement takes hold. The excitement of working toward a career goal begins to feel wasted. The uncertainty and inability to forecast the *when* drives the salesperson a little crazy inside. Their performance begins to suffer, and now when that next leadership role becomes available, you're not even considering that salesperson. Lose-lose.

Instead, set proper expectations, being transparent about the risks and uncertainties.

This sounds like: "As we grow the selling organization, there will be opportunities to pursue leadership positions. The timing and path is tough to predict, and a lot will have to do with the specific requirements for the roles. We will support you through providing opportunities to learn and grow toward the career goals you have, including leadership." Then, create periodic check-ins with your salespeople to align, update, and develop.

THE "IMMINENT EXIT" PROMISE

This promise occurs in the privately held, venture, and private equity world and sounds like, "Our plan is to build the organization up, then look to exit in one to three years." As I write this, I've been recruited three times with similar promises.

Here was one of them: "Todd, I know you're loving what you're doing, but I have an incredible opportunity for you. It's a CRO (chief revenue officer) position for a newly minted 'unicorn.' They've just taken funding at a $120 billion valuation and need someone to build and optimize so they can exit in the next 18 months."

The other two sounded almost the same.

Seventy-five percent of venture-backed companies never return cash to their investors.[35] If you're a leader hiring salespeople or hiring other leaders, this overpromise can shift a great relationship into a frustrating downward spiral of disengagement. Instead, share the exit as a goal, but remind the individual of why they are joining a company like yours. Set realistic expectations but reinforce the uncertainty. If your goal is a quick exit with a fast return, that's great—identify it as a goal, not an expectation.

THE "TOP REP PAYOUT" PROMISE

"Our top sales rep made seven figures last year." It is hard for me to fathom that this blowhard-ism approach to recruiting still exists, but it does. Recruiters and sales leaders are still using this sentence to entice future sales candidates.

In discussing the concepts of this book with other prominent sales leaders, one shared a strategy that I found to be a fantastic example of someone doing it right! During job interviews, when the subject of sales compensation comes up, this leader is ready; he plays his team's quota attainment and compensation data cards faceup. Instead of simply discussing salary and on-target earnings (OTE), he shares quota attainment numbers from the previous year.

"Last year, 64% of our account executives hit their target. That is lower than we would like, and here's what we have done to address it . . . " Transparency.

"We had two reps achieve north of 150% of their target. Here is how much they made . . . " Transparency.

"We had six reps achieve less than 50% of their target. Here is how much they made . . . " Transparency.

I have been in environments where the sales leader's leader drives hiring like old-school sales pursuits—"Just get the deal." In much the same capacity as sales pursuits, where you want clients who buy, stay, buy more, and advocate, recruiting works the same way. A focused emphasis on reducing turnover starts with the conversation above. It is not after the salesperson is hired—it is before! Set accurate expectations and consistently meet them. Build a foundation of trust.

THE "BIG PILE O' SHARES" PROMISE

"As a part of your compensation package, we're granting you a stock grant of 20,000 shares." To the average individual, 20,000 shares sounds like a lot. The problem? Our brains are terrible at understanding big numbers.

For example, imagine communicating to a new hire, "You will receive a million seconds of training here." Wow, that sounds like a lot, right? It's 11 1/2 days.

Yet, sales leaders throw these ginormous numbers at new hires without the transparent communication that sets proper expectations around their value. Without those expectations set, the brain of your salesperson may believe those shares will one day be worth $69.5 million, which is what 20,000 shares of Amazon (NASDAQ: AMZN $3,478.05) are worth as of this writing. It's the way we process big numbers, and in the process of including this in a candidate's offer, the expectation of riches becomes a draw that is soon disappointing.

Can we do a little math? At its simplest level, think about it this way. In most venture or equity-backed organizations, around 10% of available shares are reserved for the employees or other common shareholders. For fun, let's say that your company exits via acquisition for $100,000,000. That would be incredible, right? In a best-case environment, $10,000,000 becomes available for distribution to the employees. Let's imagine there were only 100 employees. If each employee had received and vested the same number of shares, the payout is $100,000 each. Still pretty darn good. However, do you think each employee has received the same number of shares? Your boss likely has quite a few more, right?

In a best-case scenario of a $100 million exit, the employee with 20,000 shares is receiving a decent car as a payout. This does not even account for the distribution of preferred versus common shareholders, but that's a more complex discussion for another day. Employees will never see a dime from those stock grants, as 75% of venture-backed companies never return a dime to their investors, either.[36]

For your salespeople to be successful, part of your role is to transfer confidence. Confidence begins with transparency, honesty, and accurate expectation setting. It's not to say that we suck, we will likely fail, and your compensation plan has no opportunity to accomplish your financial goals.

Instead, play your cards faceup. Can you . . .

- Share your plan for the business, and why you are bullish on the possibilities, while also sharing the risks?
- Share the expectations around how personal and professional growth is prioritized in the business, how those decisions are made, and the caveat that micro- and macroeconomic factors play a big role in those plans?
- Share the compensation and stock grant plan, with an explanation so an individual can truly evaluate their value? Can you add how individuals will have the opportunity to earn more shares?

The focus of the sales interview is to seek a mutual understanding of fit. Hiring a candidate is not about getting the sale. Hiring a candidate is about finding and developing mutual alignment around achieving each other's goals—both professionally and personally. With expectations properly set, sprinkled in with the unexpected honesty as described, trust is built, alignment is built, and mutual perception of fit springs from those seeds. Without trust, there can be no alignment.

In the context of intrinsic inspiration, predictability is our human drive to desire certainty. We do our best work when we can forecast what our day will look like, the results of our efforts, how those efforts will be judged, and what our interactions will likely be. Uncertainty drives us crazy, reduces engagement, and stops our brains from optimally performing. Your responsibility is to help your team forecast what their efforts, their day, their month, and their future might look like. Your responsibility to set those expectations begins before your team member's day one and never ends.

Embrace the truth and set accurate expectations to attract the right individuals who will stay, perform, and advocate.

CHAPTER 9

RECOGNITION

Whatever we have a taste for, we will be interested in; what
we really become interested in, we are bound to love, sooner
or later, and success comes from loving our work.

— Orison Marden, *Selling Things*, 1916

A S HUMAN BEINGS, WE ARE OPTIMALLY DRIVEN TO PERFORM OUR BEST
when recognition, status, and feedback are available. As individuals, we tend
to work less and for shorter periods when we feel our efforts are not acknowl-
edged and validated.

Beyond achieving personal satisfaction, the visibility of doing so is a core driver of
intrinsic inspiration. In other words, we want to be noticed. We want status. We
want to have our name in lights.

Four years ago, at the beginning of a quarter, I was thinking about ways to drive
performance earlier in the month. Like many businesses, our performance spiked
at the end of a month, especially at the quarter's end. I had an idea around how to
do it, so I tracked down our chief financial officer (CFO).

I asked, "How can we carve out budget for small gifts, awards, and bonuses that we can use to spike motivation, focus energies, and build camaraderie?"

"I'll be right back," my CFO responded.

An hour later, he walked into my office and handed me ten $100 bills in an envelope.

"Have fun!"

I gathered my vice president of sales, and together we walked into the area where all our corporate (inside) sellers were located. I announced to the team that for the next 10 deals that close where the annual recurring revenue is over $10,000, I would walk out and hand the sales rep who closed said deal one of the $100 bills with pomp and pageantry. We would list out on the whiteboard the recipients of the 10 bills.

We closed 10 deals over $10,000 in annual recurring revenue in a faster period than we had ever accomplished outside of the end of a quarter. Mind you, the average commission on such a deal for the salesperson was 8.5%. The average deal size of those 10 deals was $21,000. So, the average commission a rep received for closing a qualifying opportunity was $1,785.

The reps climbed over each other for one of the ten $100 bills. The reps would be paid, on average, 18 times that amount in commission. The trash talk taking place after the eighth deal was closed around who would fill the last two spots on the whiteboard was hilarious and amazing. Was it the $100 that drove the additional motivation extrinsically? Or was it the pageantry of the delivery of the $100 bills and their name on the board as one of the 10?

We are driven both consciously and subconsciously toward optimizing the attention we receive and the perception others have of us. We buy fancy cars that are beyond our budget to be recognized for our successes. We will take a more impressive-sounding job title to acquire said label we can tell our friends. An acquaintance of mine took a vice president of sales position for a technology company. Impressive, right? I made the mistake of asking, "How big is the organization?"

"Well, we're a startup, and I'm the only salesperson."

As individuals, this "recognition" category is broad in that it encompasses the overall coaching we seek to drive ourselves toward our goals. Still, it also includes the simple need for validation. Earlier in my career, the supply of salespeople with the proper experience levels was nearly equal to the demand. And, following the tragedy of September 11, 2001, the supply of mid-level sales managers was considerably higher than the demand. As a result, leaders could afford to drive their teams more aggressively. Leaders could afford to treat their team members as though they should be lucky they are employed and even more fortunate to be employed in their organization. However, in an economy where the supply of salespeople is so much lower than the demand, leaders practically must thank their team members for showing up each day. Validation is an appreciation for the effort, which should be considered daily.

On a weekly basis, leaders need to seek out opportunities to recognize the efforts of their team members. Beyond the "Hey, thanks for showing up again today" environment we seem to be a part of today, recognition is a public calling-out of both the positive contributions, but as mentioned in an earlier chapter, a celebration of effort for even the losses.

The first checkbox on your list, as a sales leader, of considerations for how your team members are intrinsically inspired is through recognition and feedback in the broad sense.

GIVING FEEDBACK

I am not the expert on delivering feedback, as piles of books and resources can do this subject much better justice. However, there are two considerable lessons learned that you could apply to your team environment right away that psychologically deliver the desired outcome: (1) dump the laundry list and deliver just one opportunity for improvement at a time, and (2) start with a single positive critique first.

Regarding the first lesson, when delivering a critique of a team member, deliver one positive and *only one* opportunity to improve at a time. Think about it. When receiving a laundry list of reasons why you suck, does that help you or put you on the defensive? Does it make you feel like this individual has your best interests in mind, or does it make you feel like this person thinks you suck?

As a sales leader, I once had a conversation like this with my boss. Upon arriving for our weekly one-on-one, he began the meeting by telling me how much he appreciates me and loves the progress we've made as an organization. He then proceeded to tell me, "I just spent the last hour at a Starbucks preparing for this meeting. I made a list of the 10 things I love about your work and 10 areas of potential improvement."

Ten. Of each category.

While he did begin with my second tip, delivering a positive critique first, which do you think I remembered? To this day, I remember one of the negatives and nothing else. That one negative? It had to do with what my eyes do during a difficult conversation and where I should be looking. It was ridiculous, so it stuck with me.

While delivering the list of 10, in between each one he emphatically proclaimed, "Todd, remember the 10 positives!"

To drive an individual to want to improve, avoid the list. Begin with a single positive, then deliver just one constructive opportunity to improve. Then stop. Now is not the time to move onto a second in each category. Wait a week, two weeks, a month, or some gap in time where the feedback can marinate, adjustments can be made, and the individual is ready for the next opportunity to improve.

As a sales leader, delivering feedback often drives intrinsic inspiration, too. Seek to do some form of feedback sharing and coaching at least weekly. Gallup has found that when managers provide weekly (versus annual) feedback, team members are:

- 5.2 times more likely to strongly agree that they receive meaningful feedback
- 3.2 times more likely to strongly agree they are motivated to do outstanding work
- 2.7 times more likely to be engaged at work[37]

Always remember to provide praise in public, critique in private. The concept of collecting piles of feedback, then unloading it all at once never achieves the desired result, and more often creates many unintended consequences. Consider more frequent, bite-sized deliveries of both praise and critique, and watch your team embrace and grow from it.

Titles, public recognition, and even the simple validation for showing up every day drives individuals to achieve and accomplish more than simply higher compensation. As a sales leader, consider the motivation created by recognition, seek ways to recognize your team's efforts daily, create situations where team members can achieve in a public view, and do not underestimate the power of status amongst those who achieve.

CHAPTER 10

AIM

What is the greatest cause of inefficiency? It is lack of definite purpose. This is the great tragedy of life. The man who has no definite object in life is going nowhere, he is just drifting, and that is the reason he never arrives.

— James Samuel Knox, *Salesmanship and Business Efficiency*, 1915

WE, AS HUMAN BEINGS, ARE DRIVEN BY SITUATIONS OR ENVIRONMENTS where there is satisfaction in purpose, mission, helping others, or making an impact beyond just themselves. Individuals are less likely to do their best when they feel their aim at work does not matter.

Have you been in a role or a position where you felt like you were just a cog in a machine? Where you had an employee identification number, a sales number to hit, and that was it? I know I have. I'm sure my work mattered to the company's investors somewhere. My work probably mattered to my boss, who had a number to achieve for her boss, who had a number to achieve for his boss. But does that matter?

My first technology job years ago was like that. I worked for a company notoriously known for grinding through salespeople. Yet, I managed to stay for three and a half years, which I referred to as being like dog years. You were given a target you could not possibly achieve. I finished as the number-one mid-market rep in the region, yet I achieved just 66% of my target.

We were selling software for the old mainframe computers. Mainframes are large-scale computing devices responsible for running critical processes within large companies at the time. The software we sold sat on massive computers in dedicated and protected rooms.

For as long as I stayed, the functions of this technology were so intricate, I'm still not quite sure what some of the software did for my clients.

I had friends at work, more broadly as an element of *security* to be discussed in Chapter 12. It's probably why I stayed as long as I did, and it was definitely why I left. My best friend at work left and took me with him a few months later.

Did our work really matter? Not to me, it didn't.

There are three core questions to ask yourself.

1. Do the individuals on my sales team know what their work truly means to me, both professionally and personally?
2. Do the individuals on my sales team know what their work means to our organization and our customers?
3. Do the individuals on my sales team know what their work means to the customers of our customers?

Salespeople on a mission, with a true purpose beyond just striving to hit a number, making an impact daily that is a benefit to society will achieve more. They will stay longer. They will advocate.

If you are in a business-to-business environment, your business is in business for a reason. It makes money because there are companies who pay for your services. Those companies pay for your services not for the joy of spending money, but for their benefit from making the investment. And those companies are in business to benefit others, too. It may be to benefit other companies, or it may be to benefit their customer's customers.

Do your sales reps know why companies buy from you beyond to solve business problems? When those problems are solved, how does it impact their customers?

Imagine you're selling technology that helps the efficiency of a medical device company. Individuals work in a warehouse of that medical device company manually assembling portions of those devices day in and day out. Your technology helps them do so more accurately and at a greater speed.

So what? You have a lunch-and-learn, where that customer comes in to address your sales team. However, they bring one of *their* customers with them for the event.

That customer starts in, "If it wasn't for (medical device company) and their team members assembling these devices accurately, I wouldn't be here today." That customer's children run across the cafeteria to join their parent, who is speaking.

"And I wouldn't have a mommy."

Your customer addresses your sales team. "The technology you have sold us, which we have implemented and use every single day, allows us to do this for more individuals. To keep people alive. To keep families together."

How would you feel, as a salesperson, after witnessing this interaction? Your customer. Your customer's customer. Their children. All together because of the technology your company provided. All together because your organization was able to guide the customer through a buying journey where the correct solution was matched up, purchased, implemented, maintained, and tuned to be optimized. You probably went to bed that night feeling pretty good about the company you're working for and the impact your efforts and those of your teammates are having on the world. The following day, you were probably ready to run through a brick wall to make more happy memories for individuals and their families.

This is an extreme example. However, as a sales leader, can you answer the three questions posed above for your salespeople? Do you know the answers yourself?

What would happen if your business closed tomorrow? Beyond the job losses, what would your customers' customers have to now live without? Aim isn't about profit. Aim is about meaning to your work.

One of my advisory clients, ShoppingGives, has a team of salespeople selling technology that sits on the checkout page of eCommerce sites. That's what they do—sell technology. But what are they really doing? Saving lives. Because this technology allows organizations to donate a portion of their purchase to the charity of their choosing. Massive impact, one transaction at a time.

Those examples are easy. But what about when it's not so easy?

My last company, PowerReviews, enabled retailers and brands to collect and display ratings and reviews on their websites. There is no question whether you've interacted with PowerReviews' technology at some point, probably in the past few weeks. You visit a retailer's website, browse products, click on a product page, and those reviews that appear may have been collected, moderated, and displayed by a technology like PowerReviews. What's the impact? Endless. Reviews on a website help consumers make better purchasing decisions. Those purchasing decisions impact their lives—no matter how small. The clothes people wear impact their self-esteem, sometimes their careers. The electronics people buy impact their weekends and their family time. Reviews impact where people dine, what experiences they choose to engage with, and how they spend their hard-earned dollars.

Our salespeople weren't just selling reviews technology, they were impacting people's lives every single day.

Your team's work matters beyond their number, but do they know how? During your next one-on-one with your team members, why not ask, "In what way do you think your selling efforts from (this month/this quarter) resulted in value for a customer's customer?" Are you satisfied with the answers you get? Make it your aim to align the work of your team to the outcomes of your customer's customers, and if it really matters, you'll find their intrinsic inspiration for their job rise.

STARTING OVER AT ZERO

I assign a quota to each traveler. This quota represents the
number of sales which each traveler must produce from his
territory during the period in order to maintain his standing
and to show the results we expect.

— Ricord Gradwell, Manager of Sales,
Oliver Typewriter Company, 1905

The quota, originally designed as a measure to understand whether a salesperson has paid for themselves, has evolved to a rite of passage that occurs at the beginning of every organization's new fiscal year. It's the "starting over at zero" tradition. Whatever you were measured on the previous year starts over at zero. Your quota attainment, revenue attainment, or whatever other metric your sales team is measured by, regardless of whether you attained 200% of that target or fell well short, everyone begins anew at 0%. It is a brand-new ballgame. It is eroding intrinsic inspiration.

While we may celebrate the achievers and overachievers at your annual revenue team kickoff, what happened in the past is soon forgotten. The scoreboard is erased, and those underachievers are now equal to the overachievers.

The practice of starting over at zero each year reengages and rewards your underachievers. The practice of starting over at zero each year reduces the intrinsic inspiration of your achievers and overachievers.

An age-old, never questioned practice: starting over at zero. Read the two sentences above again. The result is a reward for your bottom performers and a penalty for the top. Is it time to rethink this tradition? Absolutely.

Dan Ariely is a professor of psychology and behavioral economics at Duke University and one of my favorite follows. Ariely did a study that draws parallels to this common sales management tradition and speaks to how it is subconsciously demotivating and eroding the intrinsic inspiration of your top performers.

In the study, Dan's team brought in several participants to build Bionicles,[38] which are a type of Lego model. Each model has about 40 pieces, and the participants were asked to build them in exchange for pay. For the first model, each participant was asked if they would like to build one of the models for $3.00. Once completed, the participant would be given another model and asked if they would like to build it for $2.70. The process continued, where each model would pay $.30 less until the participant would decide to stop building, that the effort and time commitment was no longer worth the pay.

However, a second group of participants was brought in to do the same thing. They were handed a model and asked if they would like to build it for $3.00. The participant was then asked if they would like to build another for $2.70, $2.40 for the following, and so on. However, these participants had a different experience. As the participant in this second group built their second model, the first model was disassembled by the moderator right in front of the individual. The parts were put back in the original box.

The results? While each group had the same exact responsibility and the same exact compensation, the second group, who watched their work be disassembled right in front of their eyes as they worked on the next Bionicle, completed almost half of the number the first group did before giving up. Almost half!

In the sales world, are we disassembling the salesperson's work right in front of their eyes based on an arbitrary date at the beginning of the year, removing the ability for those individuals to see their results, their impact, and the fruits of their labor? Are we disassembling their intrinsic inspiration? In drawing a correlation between this study, and the statistically significant conclusion that removing the visibility of one's impact removes their emotional connection to the work, this practice of starting everyone over at zero each year is likely creating a subconscious high cost to your business.

WHERE TO START

For your sales personnel who bring new logos in the door, is it possible to create a visual for the rep to see their name associated with that account in a place where the rest of the organization can see it? Forever?

Can you give quota achievers a lower quota that following year, or start them part of the way to their target, based on their previous year's overachievement? You want those overachievers to stay, right? There's a significant cost to their leaving, right? This investment is likely worth it!

As discussed in the earlier chapter on recognition as a source of intrinsic inspiration, status and recognition do not cost you anything and have a larger impact than simply a bigger paycheck. When individuals can see their impact every day beyond their own forecast and paycheck, intrinsic inspiration grows. Coupled with making it visible for others to see, it becomes a source of pride. It becomes a source of motivation to create an even bigger impact. Make the fruits of their labor visible for all to see, and those top performers will likely stay, bring their best selves to the work each day, and advocate to others on your behalf.

Does the aim and mission of your team members matter? Are they able to see the fruits of their work in the form of impact on you, your company, your customers, and their customers? If your team is just a number with a number, and your one-on-ones are solely about the forecast and deals each week, don't be surprised when your top performers leave. Aim is the unique magnet that attracts and retains your top talent, but your top talent must know what it is and why it matters.

CHAPTER 11

INDEPENDENCE

*The man or woman who gets the farthest ahead is usually the
one who does the most good work with the least supervision.
Results will tell.*

— H.E. Eldridge, *Forbes* magazine, April 26, 1924

W E AS HUMAN BEINGS CRAVE CONTROL, AUTONOMY, AND THE TRUST of others. It is when we do our best work.

"Is that a personal call?" were five words spoken frequently as my boss slowly strolled around the six-cube farm in one of my early sales roles.

In another, I had to turn in a spreadsheet consisting of the 250 cold calls I made that week, including who I called, whether a connection was made, whether a message was left and if an appointment was scheduled.

While it is often said "I don't like to be micromanaged," that's coming from a powerful subconscious drive. Our personal freedoms drive the intrinsic inspiration to do our best work. When the opposite is true, when others control or observe most of our work, we become less engaged in our efforts.

One could argue that *independence* is the top of Maslow's hierarchy of needs. Self-actualization is summarized through the achievement of our full potential. Having control over ourselves, our ability to experiment, be creative, and control our environment is intrinsically invigorating.

As a sales leader, you have likely read the two paragraphs above and thought, "Totally agree with this one!" But, in combination with the *predictability* element discussed in Chapter 8, a conundrum is created.

Before the pandemic of 2020, the technology to execute a remote sales organization existed. In 2010, I was the vice president of global sales for a technology company headquartered in Auckland, New Zealand. I was based in Chicago. My team consisted of sellers situated worldwide, none in Chicago. We used Skype video for team calls, which was reliable at the time. We performed great. From a behavioral perspective, there's a reason why it was never more pervasive.

We are driven toward control, autonomy, and the trust of others. Remote work maximizes that feeling of control. However, as a sales leader, we are also driven to predict. We are driven toward certainty. Our struggle to predict and gain certainty is multiplied when we cannot oversee those who control our destiny—our sales teams.

Remote sales environments are great for salespeople but inherently are not great for organizational and sales leadership.

So, what happened when the pandemic forced remote work? Daily check-ins. For the weeks immediately following the initial lockdown, sales leader after sales leader engaged their salespeople in daily team calls. Some organizations were doing two per day. One to begin the day, to set the tone, with each salesperson sharing their goals for the day. The second call took place at the end of the day, where each salesperson would share what they accomplished. An hour-plus per day of lying to one another. Using your powers of empathy, imagine what a salesperson does for the half hour before the first call? They likely are spending time writing their speech. "What can I say that will appease my manager while also not sounding like a jackass to my teammates?" What is that same salesperson doing for the half hour before the second call? You can probably guess that they are doing the same thing as before the first check-in call of the day; making things up and weighing their delivery.

Time wasted. Micromanaged. More time on video. More oversight to make up for the lack of eyeballs on the actual team. It's subconscious.

Whose subconscious desires win? Well, that's up to you as a sales leader. That's part of being transparent with your team. That is creating an environment where there is alignment between the environment and culture you create while gaining alignment with your team around their role in ensuring that environment and culture can exist.

SHOWERS, STARING AT THE WALL, AND MAKE BELIEVE

You need to be creative to be successful in sales. The best sales professionals think outside the box. The best sales leaders think outside of the box, too.

Does our traditional approach to sales leadership stomp on the brains of those trying to be creative at work? Considering the office environment, when you look out across your sales team and see one of them staring aimlessly out the window, does that upset you? Would you prefer they pretend to be working when what they need is a shot of airheadedness to allow the brain to do some free association?

If you're a human being, which I'm assuming you are, you probably get your best ideas while taking a shower. There's a particular reason why. Showers are a perfect combination of three things required to create an optimized, creative brain: distractions are lowered, relaxation is maximized, and dopamine is released.

You can't force it. Your brain is less active when you are concentrating. Its gates and filters are relaxed. It's not a completely useless activity. You are accomplishing something. And that warm water splashing across your neck? It hits all three—no distractions, high relaxation, and dopamine.

So, the answer is obviously to install showers in your sales offices, right? Ummm, no.

However, people are distracting. Devices are distracting. Open office environments are productivity killers.

The open office environment was theoretically invented and celebrated in the sales world as a key instrument of motivation, collaboration, learning, and celebration. Hearing someone make a prospecting call should motivate others to pick up the phone, and listening to those conversations are potential learning experiences.

The science says otherwise.

Performing in front of other people creates anxiety. Making prospecting calls creates anxiety. Neurologically speaking, maximizing brain comfort and focus is vital to creating top performance from your selling organization.

One of the primary things that annoys your brain is a sound or conversation that you are not able to tune out and cannot predict when it will end. It's why sirens on emergency vehicles were developed—to annoy. You cannot just tune them out. Even when we have our own children, a baby crying on an airplane is almost impossible to tune out given that we cannot predict when it will end.

On the other hand, I'm writing this paragraph from a coffee shop. It's a little noisy. There is music playing from the 1960s, and it is loud. However, it's easy to tune out, and I can do my best work in this environment. What's the difference? The chatter serves as white noise to the brain because it is not relevant, and it is predictable. Two tables over, two individuals are having a conversation. Tuning in for a second, they're discussing an individual's tiny hands. While strange, the conversation is irrelevant to me, and thus easy to tune out and move on.

However, another individual picked up her phone and started a conversation. I can only hear what she is saying, not the other individual she was speaking with. The brain finds this harder to tune out because of the brain's desire to predict how individuals will react or respond. A two-way conversation is not annoying to our brain when it is irrelevant but hearing one half of a conversation is difficult.

What is annoying for the brain is *created by* open office environments. As a result, productivity goes down. Headphones go on. Collaboration is reduced. Performance suffers. Less calls get made. The sounds and conversations that others are having on the phone within earshot are impossible to tune out because of three primary reasons:

- It is potentially relevant,
- The end cannot be predicted, and,
- You can only hear one side of the conversation.

Add one more thing to the list: the best sales professionals are not afraid to make mistakes. However, even the best ones would prefer not to make those mistakes in public. And even worst, those sales professionals would not like to make those mistakes in front of their peers. The perception of being judged by others creates anxiety. Making a phone call surrounded by peers generates assumed judgment anxiety.

As sales leaders, creating an environment of autonomy, control, and free from anxiety is vital for fostering a culture of activity and productivity.

DESIGNING FOR *INDEPENDENCE*

While cube walls may seem cold, they're great for reducing selling anxiety when in an office together. Removable or retractable walls do exist. Phone booths do exist. You can schedule call blitzes and put up the walls, assign phone booths, reserve conference rooms for individuals, or encourage call blitzes to take place remotely. One chief revenue officer I spoke with has white noise coming from speakers hanging over the sales floor to drown out sounds and conversations, assisting the brain in focus.

Next, encourage your team to maximize opportunities to optimize the brain for creativity. If they are remote, encourage them to take a nature walk. Yes, I know that sounds cheesy, however, relaxation, lack of distraction, and a little dose of dopamine does the brain wonders.

Walk by yourself. Allow people to daydream. People are distracting. Devices are distracting. Much of what you're reading in this book is the result of shutting everything off, including long drives with the radio off.

As Nick Stockton of *Wired* magazine says, "Aimless engagement in an activity is a great catalyst for free association."[39]

Encourage your team to take time during the day—if not just to fuel creativity, but also to fuel overall mental health. The individuals who work in an environment where mental health is not prioritized? They have a 300% higher risk of being diagnosed with depression.[40] Working long hours has always been recognized as creating a higher risk for heart disease or stroke, and it turns out that poor leadership equals higher rates of depression. That's on you.

THE CULTURE OF LUCK

In the selling cultures you are creating, you may be surprised at the role perceived momentum and luck play in your team's performance. You'll hear your reps talk about their bad luck in certain cases. You may have reps who follow a great year with a subpar year and blame it on a loss of momentum or a string of unfortunate luck.

Multiple studies show that if you believe you are a lucky person, you are more likely to perform better than those who think they are extraordinarily unlucky. With your team, their perception of luck becomes a self-fulfilling prophecy, and as a result, impacts their performance.

One study, led by psychologist Professor Richard Wiseman, brought 400 individuals between the ages of 18 and 84 into a lab.[41] To begin, Wiseman asked each person to self-identify themselves as either "lucky" or "unlucky." He then asked these individuals to go through a newspaper and count how many photos were inside.

The self-identified unlucky group took two minutes to count the number of ads in the newspaper. However, the self-identified lucky group took only mere seconds.

Why the difference?

For all participants, on page 2 of the newspaper in large letters, it read,

"STOP COUNTING. THERE ARE 43 PHOTOGRAPHS IN THIS NEWSPAPER."

The lucky group was much more likely to notice the text on page 2. They were much more likely to notice the unexpected. It was staring them right in the face . . . and somehow, those unlucky people tended to miss it.

The multiple studies (of which the ad counting study was just one) determined that the more tense, anxious, and self-doubting you are, the less likely you are to see opportunities. The harder they looked, the less they saw!

What do you do with all this, for yourself and your team?

Engage in diagnosis: It starts with a self-diagnosing mindset. How do you deal with negative things that happen to you? How does your team deal with negative events? What is the level of anxiousness and self-doubt for the required activities to be successful? Maybe your sellers must engage in activities they don't like (i.e., prospecting), aren't optimally trained to deliver (messaging, handling objections), or don't feel a match between their personality and the task (i.e., traditional negotiations).

Reinforce new mindsets: During the downturn of 2000, followed by 9/11, I lost my job. I couldn't look past my paycheck. I then ran from job to job, solely focused on pay, putting tremendous pressure on myself to succeed, and couldn't see beyond it. That pressure didn't allow me to notice opportunities all around me. The day I started thinking about things that happened to me as "that could have been worse" instead of "wow, my luck sucks" was when opportunities started finding me.

Embrace the situation: As Einstein once said, "You don't get anywhere by not 'wasting' time." The seeds of his most famous discoveries came when he was hanging around without purpose. These last two years (2020 and 2021) have been uncertain and sometimes downright scary times; people were printing t-shirts proclaiming how badly the years suck. Remember, it could be worse.

Oh, and by the way, Einstein was "discovered" in 1921 by luck. While he may have eventually earned notoriety through his works in another way (no one can know for sure), he happened to be traveling with a Zionist leader named Chaim Weizmann. Thousands came to see Weizmann on April 3, 1921. Journalists who came to interview Einstein at the same time were surprised by the crowd. They assumed they were *all* there to see Einstein. Astonished by his popularity and not knowing all those people weren't there to see him—Einstein turned into front-page news that day.[42]

Good luck happens to those who believe in their good luck. Embrace the positive and be one of those who come out on top when this is all over—which it will be.

STEALING TIME

As a last *independence* tip, consider when you are at your best each day.

For me, I do my best work in the morning. I'm an early riser, have a healthy breakfast, do a little reading, and have established a good habit of getting to the gym four days per week from 7 am to 8 am. My most productive working time is from 8am to 11am. It's when I've written the bulk of this book, when I feel at my best delivering keynotes and workshops, and when I optimally try to schedule my most important work. It's not to say the rest of the day is less effective. However, I do hit a lull at 2 pm. Nothing a little coffee can't help, but I try to do proposals, invoicing, marketing, LinkedIn engagement, and other business tasks mid-afternoon.

As you're reading this, I hope it has inspired you to think about your own peaks and valleys during the day. More importantly, do you know the peaks and valleys of your team members?

Your team's most important asset is their time. It's of limited inventory, and once it's spent, it's gone. Peak performance time is the most valuable.

Unfortunately, I've seen many sales leaders not take the concept of peak performance time into account, and quite literally steal productivity from their team. For example, you have a team of six people. Four of them have an internal peak productivity time from 9 am to 10 am. However, you run a daily stand-up/check-in from 9 am to 9:30 am each day. Your team members leave that meeting, often with some homework to do, and must shift into productivity. That homework plus shift could take 15 minutes or longer. What have you done? At a minimum, you've just stolen 75% of the peak productivity time of 66% of your team.

During your next one-on-one with each rep, ask them for their perspective on their peaks and valleys. Most of us know or at least have a feeling as to when we consistently feel our best and accomplish our most. Most of us know or at least have a feeling about when we start to drag each day. Why not consider scheduling team meetings for most of the team's least productive time, and optimize the environment for your team during their most productive? And, at the very least, make sure you're not scheduling those one-on-ones with an individual rep during their most productive time or bothering them via Slack, text, or call.

As a sales leader, you will feel a need for your own level of control, which, without self-actualization as to your approach, can drive disengagement and a tendency to micromanage. Be aware of your own approaches to how you monitor your team's activity, encourage your team to take mind breaks, and create a culture where the mindset of luck thrives. Align with the members of your team to optimize their independence to when they do their best work. Provide the freedom for your team members to optimize each day. We all have pockets of time each day when we feel our most productive, and times we don't. As a sales leader, don't steal those productive times.

CHAPTER 12

SECURITY

*I sincerely believe that big success of a permanent nature is
never achieved by hurting anyone, by attempting monopoly or
by any kind of business organization that does not go on the
principle of co-operating with one's associates and customers.*

— Irving T. Bush, President of the Bush Terminal Company, 1921

WHAT IS WORSE, BEING LONELY OR SMOKING 15 CIGARETTES PER DAY?
According to a study, it may be about equal.[43]

We, as human beings, thrive in situations or environments where we feel
relatedness, association, and safety—where we are part of a pack. Individuals are less likely to stay and perform their best when they feel alone, at risk, and/
or where they feel as though others do not have their back.

Think about the best jobs you've had in your career. What jobs do you miss the
most? Was it the ones where you made the most money? Had the greatest opportunity to learn? Worked for the best boss? Could be. For me, thinking back to
my three favorite work experiences, when I came to work and my co-workers felt

like family (ahem . . . the family you love to hang out with, not the crazy ones), I couldn't wait to work, collaborate, stay, and perform.

Imagine, you are stranded in a jungle. You must not only provide for yourself, but you also have to survive. Would you think your production, required not only for focus but also creativity, would thrive better if you were part of a pack or all by yourself? In a pack, there's a certain level of comfort in the feeling that you simply need to be faster than one person in the group to avoid being eaten! For example, have you ever watched the television show *Survivor*? As of this writing, it's in season number 41.[44] Individuals are taken out to a remote destination, dropped in the middle of a forest or island, and forced to not only survive, but avoid getting voted off the island each week. The ultimate Survivor was the individual who was the last to be voted out. The show was specifically designed to challenge this *security* element. Individuals quickly formed packs and alliances. However, the show would continually change the rules, driving individual risk through challenging those packs. It created lying, cheating, and deceit. Those who did not fit in with others sometimes *wanted* to be voted off the show. *Survivor* was about surviving. Probably not the environment you want on your teams, right?

As a sales leader, fostering security and safety, being part of a pack, or being part of a team directly correlates to higher performance, lower turnover, and faster time to hire. Gallup, in their annual employee engagement studies, asks a simple question, "Do you have a best friend at work?" In a pre-pandemic study, the answer was sadly just 2 out of 10 employees in the United States felt as though they had a best friend at work. In Gallup's work, they identified that if an organization could just move that number up to 6 out of 10, profits could go up by 12%. And customer engagement could rise by 7%.[45]

In a remote or hybrid environment, achieving this connection becomes even harder. While we can claim that virtual happy hours, Zoom icebreakers, and Slack joke messaging achieve the same purpose, it cannot possibly to the level of being in an office together. Having coffee, going out to lunch, actual happy hours, and just plain old being in the trenches together is where true connections, feelings of being a part of a pack and developing bonds where we feel like others have our backs, are formed.

The issue of loneliness can have such profound impacts on your health, it prompted the United Kingdom Prime Minister Theresa May to appoint a minister for loneliness.[46] Loneliness raises "levels of stress hormones and inflammation, which in turn can increase the risk of heart disease, arthritis, Type 2 diabetes, dementia, and even suicide attempts." "Socially isolated individuals had a 30% higher risk of dying in the next seven years, and this effect was largest in middle age." Lonely individuals "experience decreased executive function," which has an impact on planning, decision-making, and abstract thinking.

LOOKING IN THE MIRROR

Threats to your security and feelings of loneliness get even worse as a sales leader. The role itself is inherently lonely.

The *original* definition of "social distance" refers to rank and authority—where the greater the distance, the greater the level of isolation. Transformative leaders can connect with their teams, but they are still the boss. While those same leaders may have friendships at work with peers or others, their role as a leader lends itself to not having anyone to help you make decisions. And once you do, you're the one who's accountable for those decisions.

This issue of security was a broadly recognized epidemic before the spring of 2020, which kicked off a double whammy for sales leaders:

- Economic downturns create distance between leaders and team members. As an economic climate shifts in a negative direction, that loneliness gets more pronounced. If subordinates have become friends, during a negative shift, a chasm builds, as perceptions of social connections are seen as clouding judgment.
- The remote and hybrid work environments have and will continue to exacerbate this issue. One of the many new terms from the 2020+ pandemic is the newly coined second definition of social distance, referring to the lack of

human interaction. There were no pleasantries, no popping by each other's desks, and very little interaction with peers on a social level.

As a sales leader, make sure you're addressing your own level of disconnectedness. While this may sound cheesy, find at least one person (not a family member) with whom you can talk about personal worries, issues, potential decisions, and feelings. Once you do, seek ways to make sure that's happening in your teams. Do your team members have an individual outside work they can confide in?

As a small business owner, I have a mentor who is also a dear friend, but I have built relationships with others in my space. As I'm writing this, I have been texting with two of them in a group, talking about our favorite bands. While it's not in person, it's connection building. We have each other's backs.

This individual doesn't have to be a mentor; have someone who's at any level. Just make sure you find someone.

Building connections that go deeper than simply your day-to-day responsibilities may sound soft, but the alternative is a lack of cognitive function, which clouds performance—or considerably worse, leads to physical illness and depression. With your teams, it will cloud their performance, create turnover, and, if packs have been formed, it may create turnover in big chunks.

MAXIMIZING SECURITY

There are three core ways to build and maximize the feeling of security between your team members. At the highest level, there's simply hanging out. The connection between team members gets deeper when they can have shared experiences together. When you can combine hanging out and sharing experiences with having shared goals, the opportunity to maximize this feeling can be achieved.

Hanging out: When I think of the bond I have with my wife, kids, and my best friends, we could literally sit on a couch doing nothing and have a blast together. Taking that to the working environment is much the same. Spending time in the trenches together, hanging out, talking about our weekends, what we're binging on television, or simply joking around connected us. Chats in the office kitchen area, heading out to lunch, grabbing coffee, or going to happy hour after work created bonds that I still have today from my first jobs years ago.

Those opportunities to build strong bonds are much more difficult in a virtual environment. For co-workers you've never actually met in person but only over video, do you think you could accurately guess how tall each of those individuals is? I have had a few surprises myself recently.

As sales leaders, are you creating opportunities for these bonds to build? Are you providing opportunities for your team members just to hang out?

A place to start building could be the lens by which you view the purpose and agenda of your sales meetings, regardless of if they are virtual, hybrid, or in person. There's an opportunity to use the valuable inventory of time associated with your weekly meetings, expanding the typical agenda beyond the traditional updates and forecast.

Sales meetings with the following four elements provide an opportunity to maximize the bonds that can take place:

1. Fun: In each and every sales meeting I hosted, you could count on an icebreaker before anything substantive was to be discussed. Even if the icebreaker took 20 minutes of the allocated hour, the benefits to the team, and even to me, were priceless.
2. Recognition: Every week, time was spent on feedback, validating the entire team and recognizing those publicly who were standing out.
3. Education: If you're not getting better, you're likely getting worse. What simple things could we teach to make each team member a little better at what they do this week?
4. Motivation: Spend a little time ensuring everyone on the team knows the impact they are making on each other, on me, on the organization, on our customers, and on our customers' customers.

Keep in mind, the best way to foster team connectivity—feelings of being in a pack and for those individuals to feel like they have each other's back—is to encourage these interactions to take place *without you*, the sales leader, involved in every one of them. You are still their manager. The dynamic shifts when you are involved versus when you are not. If you're running a virtual sales meeting, end it 15 minutes early but encourage the team to stay on and hang out. If you're still doing virtual happy hours, take it easy to ensure they are not overdone and your team members don't feel it to be an obligation. However, choose to skip those interactions and transparently explain to the team why you don't attend. Hanging out with the boss changes the dynamic of the interaction and changes the outcome.

Shared experiences: Do you have stronger bonds with the individuals you went through new hire onboarding with than others on your team or organization? Do you have strong bonds with the individuals you attended conferences with, partnered with at company events, or partnered with on strategic projects?

Experiences beyond the simple act of hanging out create stronger bonds. Seek opportunities to create experiences with your team. In a virtual environment, can you do small team-building exercises? In an in-person setting, can you plan an off-site to do some charitable work? How about attending a sporting event? Some of my strongest relationships with my sales leadership team peers from my days at ExactTarget were built via our leader's coordination of having us all attend a Chicago Cubs baseball game each year. The experience and the interactions drove deeper connections. I have no recollection of who the Cubs played or who won, but I remember the experience with my peers years later. I find baseball games to be ideal—warm weather, limited need to engage in every moment of the game.

Shared goals: Let's go back in time for a moment—back to the year 1911. You are a sales leader. You have a team selling your goods across the city, state, or even the country. It's a bit ironic considering today's challenges of remote sales leadership, considering original sales leadership was entirely done remote.

Your salespeople are not in the office in the morning. There are no Zoom check-in meetings. Your salespeople aren't engaging in any telephone prospecting, given that phones were in no way pervasive yet. They weren't in the office setting appointments, emailing from their laptop. Your reps are out in the field, selling business to business, door to door, town to town. They're not taking a daytrip to New York, where they'll be back in tomorrow. They're taking trains to different cities. Slowly. Gone for the week. Or they may even live there.

With that in mind, how would you even manage them? How would you coach them? How would you . . . communicate with them?

No CRM system.

No email.

No mobile phones.

No Slack.

Sales, for the hundreds of years before it, was a commission-only environment. It had to be. As a salesperson, it was you against the world. As a sales leader, you had to trust that your salespeople were extrinsically motivated—primarily by dollars. There were no quotas for those individuals. Salespeople representing goods honestly and ethically had a job if they wanted one. The cost of carrying a commission-only rep was minimal. When they sell something, they make a hefty commission. Salespeople loved it—they were purely independent and paid for what they sold. Commission percentages were anywhere from 33% to 40%, so there was no lack of motivation. There was no 401K or savings plans. The priority wasn't to pay for today's bills. It was to maintain a standard of living, plus saving against "old age or disability." The opportunity was real in sales in a commission-only role.

Established salespeople loved the commission-only model. But sales leaders did not.

First, salespeople continued to fall into the trap of "sell and go," meaning there was little incentive to ensure the goods purchased were delivered and used properly.

Second, as sales leaders were hiring many salespeople to meet growth objectives, commission-only meant salespeople selling under their standard of living for a considerable amount of time, which leads to a lack of patience, a lack of job satisfaction, and a lack of efficiency—three things required to be successful.

This led to their version of the salary-plus-commission environment . . . but in this environment, salary is simply another term for what we might call a recoverable draw, meaning, a rep is paid a salary, but their commissions are paid up against it—then benefits once those commissions exceed the salaried amount.

Quota and quota achievement was solely about bringing in enough revenue to pay for yourself—your salary and the expenses associated with you being in the employ of the company.

Sales in the modern sense was born as an individual sport. Today, over 110 years later, we continue to take the lessons from a different time in the way we cast judgment, recognition, and compensation to our salespeople.

I'm not arguing for changing the model entirely, as salespeople with individual territories but a team goal may turn against one another. The top performers, counting on bottom performers for part of their targeted earnings do not typically handle a team-compensation environment well, and you don't want to penalize your top performers. However, team goals galvanize packs, bring individuals together, and form bonds that are difficult to break.

I am also not talking about regular team bonding events, like escape rooms and company Jeopardy against the other functions in your organization. Instead, rally your team around hitting certain targets, with a special reward for hitting stretch goals. In my previous companies, we established extreme stretch goals with insane rewards for achieving them. One was called The Hunt. As a startup, our board target was $650, 000 as a team. For fun, we established a $2 million team stretch target, writing it on the whiteboard, discussing ideas for the reward. We laughed our way through the quarter, had some hysterical ideas, and finished the quarter at $1.3 million. But, more importantly, those first three months together glued us together. Seven years later, that original team is still in a text group together, where not a week goes by without some form of chatter.

Think beyond the individual, and create team stretch goals. They galvanize teams together as the third most effective way to build security.

Feeling alone or out on your own drives us to seek safety and security—a security found by being a part of a pack where we stay and thrive. Environments with the strongest teams, where everyone feels as though someone has their back and they have a connection with one another, directly correlates with higher performance and lower turnover. And don't forget, being a sales leader can quickly become lonely, where instead of being a part of the team, your changed responsibilities, power, and goals make you the boss. Being the boss can be a lonely place. Seek opportunities to build your packs, within your organization or through others in similar positions outside of your organization.

CHAPTER 13

EQUITABILITY

In good territories, sales(people) are overpaid;
in bad territories, they are so underpaid that
they become discouraged.

— John G. Jones, *Sales Management*, 1930

AT SOME POINT IN YOUR LIFE, YOU'VE PROBABLY SCREAMED, "THAT'S not fair!" As a child, that's a phrase repeated during games played and chores requested. At least it is at my house. As adults, our brain's radar is wired to be aware of the perceived equitability of everything.

Our equitability radar constantly assesses whether the juice is worth the squeeze, and whether everyone around you is receiving the same reward for the same output. When either is out of whack, intrinsic inspiration drops.

The reward? We have gotten this far in the book and not talked much about variable compensation, bonuses, and overall pay. Equitability comes about through the fairness of monetary rewards balanced with the intrinsic inspiration categories such as predictability, recognition, aim, independence, and security.

The effort and output are what we give up in order to get all that *rewardy goodness*. How much energy, time, and resources do I put out as an individual to receive such a reward? Do I have monetary investments I need to make to receive these rewards, paying for the cost to commute, upgrading my wardrobe, or paying for day care? Could they be home-office expenses? What is the tradeoff?

Like our children's perceptions, the second we feel like there are politics, favorites, or others receiving a larger reward for an equal or lesser effort and output, our brains start to go a bit crazy.

The office brownnoser gets all the recognition. The boss's buddy is first in line for the promotion. A peer is making more money and received a larger stock grant than you with the same job and same experience. When the effort is no longer worth the reward, we quickly find it difficult to turn on our brains for the task at hand.

We experience equitability just about every day. I recently bought a new book of business checks for my business. One book of checks. The cost was $49.99, and to make matters worse, at checkout, they wanted to charge me $14.99 for shipping and handling.

The answer to the problem of perceived unfairness becomes an issue of transparency. What you perceive to be equitable may not be how others perceive it. And when it comes as a surprise and missing expectations, disengagement occurs, where our inspiration to keep going dissipates. Sharing your approach, decision criteria, and process early and often settles the perceptions. With the check printing cost and surprise shipping add-on, are those dollar amounts fair? I don't know, but it sure didn't *feel* fair. Maybe there is a reason why this stack of paper checks should cost so much. Because it has to do with money and security? Maybe there is a reason why this stack of paper checks should also cost so much to send in the mail—not even via priority mail? Could it be the security requirements of shipping paper checks? Could they have led with those items, keeping me on the site through to purchase? By not providing any explanation or warning, the feeling of unfairness drove me to choose another path, do more research, and find an alternative.

THE PERILS OF BRINGING PEOPLE BACK INTO THE OFFICE

"Should we require our team to be in the office?" The answer to this question isn't as easy as you might think. Putting myself back in the shoes of a chief revenue officer (CRO), there are plenty of knee-jerk responses I could have:

- "Yes, for the sake of relationships, culture, and for the sake of our eyeballs that have been staring at the little green dot next to the camera on our laptops for hours per day, come on back!"
- "Wait, but this remote environment is working. We've established normalcy in it, and some people are thriving in it. Stay home if you want to!"

Taking off my CRO hat and putting on my nerd-alert behavioral science hat instead, things get murky quickly. Both of those answers are fraught with danger.

Don't *just let* the process of bringing your salespeople back into the office happen on its own. Without a plan, the chances of destroying your team member's perception of *equitability* are highly likely with both those who come back and those who don't.

Having a single policy where it's either "we're all back in" or "we're all back out" is a challenge. Now you're thinking, "maybe we make it optional," where it becomes up to the reps, but what will their answer be?

Their answer will largely depend on the seller's inherent personality. Some may be thriving in this remote environment, and others dream of the day they get to go back to the office every day.

The office environment for salespeople is biased toward extroverts. These extroverts are people who feed off the energy of others. They like to talk through ideas out loud, brainstorm, and strategize informally around just about everything.

Remote work favors introverts. These introverts do best when they have uninterrupted focus and don't feel as though others are looking and listening as they're making calls and working their opportunities.

If you make it optional, be prepared for the different personalities to select different options best for them. This may be ideal—you're making everyone happy. But are you? In so doing, you may be creating two other issues . . .

EXPECTATION INFLATION

Back in 2014, when I joined startup PowerReviews initially as their SVP of sales, things were lean. When you would come into the office, if you wanted a drink from the kitchen, you grabbed it from the refrigerator and put $.50 in a jar next to it.

Fast-forward two years. Not only did we now have multiple refrigerators filled with free drinks, we had just installed a cold-brew coffee tap. It became all the rage . . . I literally took a picture of my first cold brew from it, August 10, 2016. It was delicious. I was hooked!

Fast-forward two months. The cold-brew tap was unexpectedly out. It was empty. And there was no immediate remedy. It had become part of all of our routines, and it wasn't hard to overhear employees mumbling, "The cold-brew is out. What the f . . . ?!? Do I have to go to Starbucks now?"

Let's take this concept over to the switch from commuting to working from home.

Prior to Covid, commuting to and from work has been a necessary component of the job . . . just like dropping $.50 in the drink jar. It's just what you do. It's an element of compliance. While some organizations offered a commute perk or two, you paid for it yourself as an employee. Even if it was paid for, you still had to do it.

In the pandemic, you're not commuting. You're not braving the two-hour roundtrip. You're not getting a face full of the sweaty guy on the train. You do not have to dress like a Sherpa to get in on a lovely January day. It's been like getting that new cold-brew machine.

What you've experienced is something I like to call expectation inflation. Once we've received an additional perk, no matter how out of the ordinary versus others it is, taking it away reduces our overall satisfaction. Our expectations of normalcy have been inflated.

Once you raise the benefit expectation bar, lowering it back to where it was, even if that level is considered normal, is a lowering of satisfaction, which lowers intrinsic inspiration, which can reduce performance.

If you make coming back optional, will those who thrive in an office environment lose engagement due to a perceived unfairness of the investment required to commute?

Will they perceive those who don't come back differently, fracturing the team?

Will there be a mutiny once the commutes start coming back?

Will sellers coming back to the office require some other concession?

How will you foster a team if some employees do come back regularly, and some stay home?

DISTANCE BIAS

As our sales organizations grow, we now need to create leaders, and our desire is to promote from within, right? Who will rise to the top? How will you decide?

Subconsciously, do you think you'll lean toward the person who is always there, in the office, a clear fixture in the office culture? Or will you lean toward the person who isn't there, who may be more qualified but isn't present?

There's potential for a strong case of subconscious bias to appear in the hybrid environment. A bias toward the individuals who are in the office. You are likely to have a distance bias[47] because "We prefer people or things closer in space or time than what's farther away." It's a shortcut our brains take. In thinking back to our *predictability* element of intrinsic inspiration, our ability to predict the effectiveness of an individual in a new position is biased by the volume of interactions and proximity.

The experts I read are almost entirely predicting that a hybrid environment is here to stay, where remote work will play a vital role in the future of organizational cultures. Each of your organizations will need to be aware of both expectation inflation and distance bias, have a plan for both, and a willingness to share that plan with the individuals living in it.

Equitability is maximized through transparency and empathy. If we are not aware of the subconscious issues we create ourselves as sales leaders and are happening inside the brains of our team members, turnover will go up, performance will go down, and your ability to hire will become more challenging than it needs to be.

PART THREE

MYTHS AND APPLICATIONS

CHAPTER 14

THE THREE MYTHS OF MOTIVATION

You can't run [a salesperson] as you'd run an elevator or an automobile. It's a matter of treating the sales[person] as you would like to have [the salesperson] treat you, if under any circumstances you two changed places.

— W. C. Holman, *The Business Philosopher Magazine*, 1909

SALES LEADERS, BE CAREFUL IN YOUR ATTEMPTS TO ADD CATEGORIES to what truly drives the intrinsic inspiration of your teams. Still today, in sales organizations around the world, leaders are practicing techniques they believe will drive their teams to work harder and perform better. However, in many cases, it's driving the opposite.

The three most prominent ways sales leaders have attempted to motivate their team to stay, perform, and advocate in many cases cause the opposite impact. While they may sound counterintuitive, those three are the following:

1. Over indexing on the belief that investing in more **learning and development** for their teams will keep those individuals from leaving,

2. **Fear** motivates people, but its use in sales organizations is wholly misplaced, and,

3. Trying to win the hearts and minds of their team through benefits and **perks**.

LEARNING AND DEVELOPMENT

Imagine you've been in a role for over a year. You are considering a new position with a new company. Do you believe you will learn more in the first six weeks of that new job or in the next six weeks in your current job?

While working with several sales leaders across multiple industries during a period of high turnover, the comment is often made, "They'll stay if they are continuing to learn new skills and make investments in the rest of their career."

This may sound quite counterintuitive, but continued learning will *not* be the reason your salespeople stay. It will contribute to them not leaving. There's a difference.

It is true that when learning slows, engagement slows along with it. Learning helps individuals achieve higher levels of *recognition* via performance and improved status, and helps individuals achieve greater *independence* through added personal resources. A lack of opportunities to learn and improve will likely cause your salespeople to feel like they are coasting, starting the clock on their eventual departure.

Learning in their current job won't be *the* reason they stay. You cannot compete with new-job learning.

Continue making investments in your team, however, and your magnetism as an organization will be in balancing the six elements that drive intrinsic inspiration—the feelings that drive individuals to show up, do their best, stay, and advocate.

FEAR

Throughout my career, I've worked with and for leaders who embrace fear as a motivator. I discussed my first real sales job out of college back in Chapter 6, selling overnight shipping while living in Southern California. Daily, the hatchet of being fired swung subconsciously above my head and the heads of my teammates. We were threatened regarding daily activities, weekly performance, being in the office at certain times at the beginning and end of each day, and even the appearance of our clothing, our cube office, and our car.

During those eight months, I worked hard. I drove 24,000 miles in six months. But I was miserable. I lasted eight months in that role, and left homesick, out of shape, tired, and in debt.

Fear *is* an effective motivator. It makes us uncomfortable. If you're paddling a boat and there's a shark on your tail, you will be highly motivated to row like you've never rowed before. Fear of failure, specifically, can be just as effective. In other words, fear pushes you to solve for whatever situation you do not want.

Fear is also very effective at deteriorating your health, your relationships with others, and your IQ. Being in a state of failure has been shown to reduce the IQ of those living within it by as much as 45%.[48]

It creates emotion that is based in something negative, which drives us toward safety and something positive. Creating an environment where fear is used as a means of driving intrinsic inspiration is an effective way to drive high turnover and dramatically lower performance. And due to the proliferation of reviews on employee experience permitting every corner of the professional world on sites like Glassdoor and RepVue, it also lowers recruiting effectiveness and time to hire. As a sales leader, it will rapidly teach you the ins and outs of the unemployment system, dealing with demotions and social isolation.

PERKS

"We've got it covered. We sent her some logoed socks."

"We have a Ping-Pong table, a pop-a-shot, beer on tap, an on-site gym, . . . "

The discussion in Chapter 13 around expectation inflation extends to your perks. An added benefit today is an expectation tomorrow. In the war on talent, you will not win by simply adding more logoed company swag. You will not inspire people beyond the short term by trying to out-benefit other companies. In so doing, you may get yourself into trouble.

In one company employing around 150 at their headquarters, the in-office employee benefits were amazing. Four refrigerators filled with food, snacks, and cold beverages. Multiple drinks on tap including cold-brew coffees, beers, and even white wine. Fourteen bins filled with different snacks ranging from chips to trail mix and popcorn. Bowls of fruits like apples and avocados on the kitchen area table. Two top-end Ping-Pong tables. The building had a beautiful rooftop deck with 360-degree views around the city, and a gym with all the latest equipment.

As the organization began the process of raising an additional round of investment, the finance team presented some concerning numbers to the senior leadership team in preparation. The organization was spending between $25,000 to $30,000 per month just on food for the kitchen. The CEO decided. It's time to cut back *a little* on the kitchen area food. He did a great job of communicating the why: "We need to improve our profitability in the short term, which will allow us to take on an investment at a favorable valuation, which helps the value of all of your stock grants. The additional investment will also allow us to more rapidly accomplish the vision you all have been working so hard to achieve."

Being a transparent CEO, at each quarter's "all hands" meeting, where company and department updates are shared and individuals are recognized for their accomplishments, he would collect anonymous questions and comments from the employees. He would then read them in front of the group. The next "all hands" took place less than a month after the announcement of the cutbacks on the insane food spending.

The CEO read to the group one of the anonymous comments from one of the employees, "The lack of avocados in the kitchen area is a clear representation of the direction this organization is headed."

Do you know of any organization where you could eat three square meals per day in their kitchen? Do you know of any that even have a bowl of fresh avocados in the kitchen each day? Well, the lack of avocados created a mini mutiny.

You will not win if you are putting your focus on employee perks and swag. Set the bar. Transparency crushes perks. Embrace what you, as an organization, give up to be great at your core.

CHAPTER 15

THE APPLICATION

One must do, to know. It's not enough to
passively receive an idea; if it is really to be
yours, you must put it into act.

— James Samuel Knox, *Salesmanship and Business Efficiency*, 1915

THROUGHOUT HISTORY, THE IMPORTANCE OF SALES LEADERSHIP depended on the importance of the salesperson to an organization's success. In other words, who needs a sales manager or a sales leader in times when the product sells itself?

There are times when the economy is booming. Sales leaders have two core jobs to bring revenue in the door: recruit and report. The primary focus is on getting and keeping a performing sales team and predicting the future through a forecast. When the economy is not booming, the job of sales leadership becomes five-fold, requiring a disciplined foundation. Embracing a structure for sales leadership allows you to extend your lead in the good times and continuing to grow in the bad. That foundation can be the Five F's.

THE FIVE F'S

Let's start by reviewing and internalizing the Five F's of Maximizing Revenue Capacity. If you'd like, I can wait while you take the next 10 minutes to memorize them.

1. **Focus**
2. **Field**
3. **Fundamentals**
4. **Forecast**
5. **Fun**

Got it?

You are now miles ahead of your peers. When the bullets start to fly, you will always have this structure and way of thinking to fall back on.

ONE-ON-ONE MEETINGS

There is no better opportunity to put all the elements from this book into optimal usage than through weekly one-on-ones. For your direct reports, do them. Do them weekly. Don't miss them. Don't deprioritize them.

You're doing them already, you say? Great! The next step is to look at the content and execution of those one-on-ones. If your current one-on-ones with your direct reports are all and only about deals, pipeline, and forecast, you're doing them wrong.

Starting immediately, either when you take your first sales leadership position or you've been in the role for years, here is my recommendation:

Step 1: Schedule a weekly recurring 45-minute one-on-one meeting with each of your direct reports.

Step 2: Create a shared document. We used Google Docs. This document will be private between you and the individual.

Step 3: The Five F's become the agenda. Write the date of the first one-on-one that will be taking place, and under it write the Five F's. I used to flip "Fun" to the top, so the document would simply look like this:

TODD & STACY
1-ON-1 DOC

February 22nd

FUN:
SS notes
TC notes

FOCUS:
SS notes
TC notes

FIELD:
SS notes
TC notes

FUNDAMENTALS:
SS notes
TC notes

FORECAST:
SS notes
TC notes

The agenda for your one-on-one is already created. You'll plan to discuss and connect on fun first, then discuss any items or topics related to territory focus, then discuss tools and resources utilization or needs in the field, followed by a discussion on professional and personal development in fundamentals, followed by a discussion on deals, strategy, and key performance indicators (KPIs) in forecast. Categorize everything you could possibly need to talk about while broadening the lens beyond just the deals.

Step 4: As things come up during the week which are important but not urgent to be discussed, drop them into the shared document. By doing so, you will reduce the number of one-off meetings needed during the week, the number of interruptions, the number of Slack messages to attend to, and, instead, you have a place to collect them.

Step 5: Make sure you spend a couple of minutes before the one-on-one reading what your rep put into the doc during the week and adding any of your own notes.

Step 6: As described above, this document becomes your agenda and a place to take notes and memorialize the conversation and action items.

Step 7: Once complete, push this week's agenda and notes down, and create the Five F's agenda again for the following week. Repeat.

Not every subject needs to be covered every week, of course. However, the one-on-one structure forces you and your team members to think beyond just their deals, numbers, and their forecast each week. Are they focused on the right companies and the right individuals? Do they have the right tools and resources in the field? Is there an opportunity to coach them on their fundamentals or solicit their thoughts on where they desire more help? And perhaps most important, these one-on-ones are for the individual team member, not just for you. Starting with a discussion on the fun topics, ensuring you're mutually optimizing and recognizing issues with their own intrinsic inspiration.

Maybe you feel like one-on-ones are the least important meetings of the week. When done right using the Five F's structure, you'll find unexpected benefit. For example, you will quickly find the frequency and need for random, one-off needs for meetings shrinks, saving you time in your week. Your team members' intrinsic inspiration, and therefore their engagement and performance, will rise. They'll be able to predict as consistency matters. If you get beyond the deals and the forecast in those discussions, their feeling of security will rise. You will have more opportunities to discuss and reinforce the aim of their efforts, validate their work, and provide feedback. Conversations with the entire team are nice, but when an individual rep can look their leader in the eyes and understand that their work matters, passion and meaning blossom.

Once you start using this structure, you'll likely push it upward, too, and use it to prepare for your one-on-ones with your boss, and even skip level to their boss. I sure did . . .

HANDLING HIGH-STAKES CONVERSATIONS

It was the summer of 2009. I had been in my role serving as the vice president of worldwide sales for an initially small tech company headquartered in the Valley for probably 18 months. We were one of the lucky organizations, having survived the Great Recession. This economic downturn had devastating effects on the entire world's economies, having its most significant impact on banking and real estate. However, all industries were affected, and the data suggests it was the largest period of economic decline since the Great Depression in 1930.[49]

We survived so spectacularly, I was honored to win the American Business Stevie Award in a ceremony at Caesar's Palace in Las Vegas that January, taking home the prize for Worldwide Vice President of Sales of the Year.

Our success led to a capital raise in early 2009. Today, when a company secures a Series B, C, D, and so on, there is tremendous excitement, envy, and celebration. LinkedIn posts proclaiming the good news followed by hundreds of "Congratulations" comments, clapping hands emojis, and discussions throughout industries that include the words, "Wow! They are doing great!"

If you are in any sort of revenue leadership capacity within an organization, a fundraise opens the door to opportunity. However, a fundraise also opens the door even wider to heat. The temperature suddenly goes up in your leadership kitchen. The pressure goes way up to perform, seeing as those investors are providing growth funding to you and your organization based on a prediction of future performance. The best advice I can give you is, *"Don't miss your first-quarter forecast following a fundraise."*

Unfortunately, that is exactly what we did. After a long string of blasting through targets, the new targets were considerably higher following the raise. In the April-through-June quarter, we finished at just 94% of our forecast.

While recovering from the quarter and readying for the 4th of July holiday, which would be taking place in two days, the phone rang. It was my CEO, Michael.

"Todd, we need you to fly out today. Bob [our lead investor/chairman] needs to meet with us at the office in Menlo Park, California, at 8 am tomorrow. It'll be you and me, plus Bob . . . and they're bringing in a forensic sales expert. This expert is Bob's go-to, who is an expert at diagnosing sales and revenue holes. Be prepared to have every element of your sales organization, philosophy, and approach dissected the entire morning."

He wasn't kidding. I packed my bags and grabbed an expensive flight from Chicago to San Jose. Michael picked me up at the airport, and we proceeded to spend the rest of the evening preparing. That preparation was grounded in the Five F's. I knew that preparing based on those elements meant that every hole would be addressable. There could not possibly be any gotchas, and I was able to sleep that night.

The morning of July 3, Michael and I arrived at the venture capital firm's offices and were led to a conference room in this beautiful, almost Frank Lloyd Wright–style building. Bob (the chairman and primary investor) sat next to the "forensic sales expert," Mike, on one side of the table. Michael nor I had ever met Mike—but it was clear he was fully qualified for the role he had that morning.

Bob started in. "Todd, we just raised a substantial investment in (your organization) and promptly missed the first-quarter number. That's a problem. As such, we have allocated the next four hours to look at every aspect of your go-to-market strategy to figure out what happened and make sure we have the right people in place to maximize this investment."

Oh, good. This should be fun. And fun it wasn't.

Mike then proceeded to endlessly pummel me with questions. Every question led to another, which was exhausting, and at times frustrating. Using the Five F's framework, I was able to dictate the conversation. Mike wasn't expecting a framework. Mike also wasn't expecting my level of confidence, which wasn't cockiness (if I do say so myself). It was a confidence built on a solid-ground agenda.

- We discussed every region: the targeted accounts by geography, by vertical, by size, and by prerequisite (i.e., the focus).
- We discussed the field in excruciating detail, providing a diagnosis of every single rep's positives, opportunities for improvement, and what drives them. We dove into the tools and resources in place today and how they are used.
- We discussed the sales process, our messaging and positioning, our pricing strategy and negotiation approach, and where investments needed to be made in terms of fundamentals.
- We dove into metrics and all our key performance indicators (KPIs). We worked through the current pipeline, and together thought through what a true forecast should be.
- We finished by talking about my management style, my approach to driving engagement, and oversight given that our entire sales team was enterprise level (big deals, multiple buyers, long sales cycles), older than I was, but an even bigger deal at the time, all remote (i.e., the fun).

My CEO wasn't allowed to provide much input unless asked directly. This was about vetting me as a sales leader.

At around 11:30 am, the sales expert completed his investigation.

He looked at the chairman and said words that will forever be stuck in my head. I get chills just writing this, as Mike was a total badass.

"This guy is world-class."

The euphoria of that diagnosis lasted less than 10 seconds.

Bob, the chairman, looked at Michael (the CEO)—stared at him. I swear the stare Bob gave Michael will forever stay with me. It was though he was looking through him, into his soul. He then spoke, staring at Michael, but addressing me. "Todd, please leave the room. Have a seat in the lobby."

I knew what was about to happen, and I was practically in tears about it. My CEO, who listened to me, supported me, always had my back, and gave me my first shot at sales leadership, was about to be identified as the cause of the miss. I knew it.

Twenty minutes later, Michael walked out of the conference room quietly.

"Let's go," Michael said.

There were no pleasantries as we walked out of the investor's offices. Just Michael and me. He was clearly shaken. Suddenly, one dumb joke by one of us (I don't remember who), and the glass jar of pressure broke. We laughed like school kids—hysterically—for what felt like 10 minutes.

That experience changed me. My confidence. My perspective on leadership. No doubt that it changed the rest of my career. There is also no doubt that I would not have been prepared without a framework. And I know, to this day, that the world-class designation assigned to me by Mike would not have been earned without it.

YOUR 30/60/90-DAY PLAN ON DEMAND

How many times have you asked or have been asked, "Do you know of a good template for building a 30/60/90-day plan?" Once you've memorized and internalized the Five F's, you always have one in your brain, ready to verbalize or put on paper.

Picture this: You're being interviewed for a sales leadership role, and you're asked, "How would you go about tackling the first 30, 60, 90 days of your tenure in the role?"

If the interview is taking place virtually, your answer could be delivered verbally. However, even better, during a face-to-face interview, you could grab a piece of paper and simply write out the Five F's.

As discussed in the introduction, back in 2014, I was intrigued by a role that had opened up with a Chicago-based technology company. It was a chance to build a revenue engine from the ground up, with a solidly built foundation, a strong leader, and right in my backyard. The retained search representative informed me that they had already churned through 12 other sales leadership candidates, a couple of which I knew, and I knew they were fantastic leaders.

A half day of interviews was scheduled with their current senior leadership members. In at least three of the interviews, this question was asked. In each case, I answered using the Five F's.

"Well, I developed a framework for how I think about sales leadership. It may sound cheesy, but I call it the Five F's of Maximizing Revenue Capacity. It helps me plan, see the holes, strategize, and communicate a plan. Here goes . . .

"The first F is focus. I would want to spend time understanding the value proposition, the current customers, look at the metrics around deal sizes, win rates, cycle lengths, etcetera, and begin to establish an understanding of the company traits and individual traits of those we truly want to target, and those we don't.

"The second F is the field. In the first week, I want to sit down with every existing team member and get to know them. I would also want to access the tools and resources that are in place. From there, we would together apply the focus to developing our strategy around continuing to build and scale the pieces that will take the field each day.

"The third F is the fundamentals. Through the discussions with the field, I'll get a sense of where everyone is fundamentally, and I want to begin to teach right away. In the first sales meeting, I want them to learn something new. We'll then work on both identifying and filling the gaps between where we are and where we consistently need to be.

"The fourth F is the forecast. There's likely no time to delay. I'll want to jump into the forecast, the metrics, the pipeline, the existing opportunities, all while also assessing the way we predict. I have strong opinions on how to predict the future through the right KPIs, and the right lens by which we assess pipeline, so over time, we'll match the current approach with a future approach.

"Last, and not least, is the fifth F—fun. Creating an environment where team members want to stay, truly show up every day, and do their best, loving what they do, who they do it with, and who they do it for is key to maximizing performance. Something that starts day one and never ends is a focus on intrinsic inspiration. It will begin with the discussions with the current team members, but the output is a culture that impacts every discussion with prospects, customers, recruits, team members, partners, and so on."

Now, imagine you answer the question like this . . . in your own words? It rolls off the tongue once you have internalized the framework. In this case, being the thirteenth individual in line for the role, I had an offer within days. It doesn't mean I'm any better than any of the other candidates. But it does mean that having a plan helps their buying brain to predict. In this case, the buyers were who would become my peers. Also in this case, they were able to quickly predict what working with me would be like, and they would not have to worry about me ensuring our revenue engine was sufficiently optimized.

Once in the role, you always have a plan ready. Here's your template:

	FOCUS	FIELD	FUNDAMENTALS	FORECAST	FUN
1st 30 APPRAISAL					
2nd 30 FOUNDATION					
3rd 30 EXECUTE & MEASURE					

The Five F's across the top. Along the left side are the time windows. For a new role, the plan would be to spend some time appraising each category. What is our current focus, how are we aligned with our field, where do our fundamentals need work, how good do we feel about our forecast, and are we maximizing fun? The next 30 days? Building the foundation through prioritization of what needs to be optimized and planning it out. The third 30 days? You will spend it implementing the foundational plan and measuring the impact. Simple, on demand, and always ready to go. No stones left unturned. Make it your own, as my template isn't the prettiest in the world.

DUE DILIGENCE

Due diligence is the term for doing a comprehensive appraisal of a business. It's typically done when considering making a purchase or a significant investment to determine its potential. I used this structure quite a few times for that purpose. However, what about when you're considering the next step in your sales leadership career. The ability to uncover everything necessary to align your career with this incredibly important decision is a valuable opportunity to use the framework. Can you use the framework to have an endless number of questions about the company's go-to-market, and specifically, the role? Of course, you can!

WHAT QUESTIONS DO YOU HAVE ABOUT THE POSITION?

The first F is focus, so begin your questioning there.

- When the sales team and the marketing team wake up each morning, how do they prioritize the companies and individuals they will focus on?
- What are the firmographics of the companies that constitute the shortest path to the most valuable opportunities?
- What individuals within those organizations do they think about, learn about, and target?

Then, proceed to questions around the field. Based on that focus, how have you thought about deploying resources into the field?

- What's a typical profile of salesperson here? Why?
- How are they supported internally? Revenue operations? Enablement? Other?
- What tools make up the stack used to optimize their efforts?

Next, you could dig into the fundamentals.

- Given the organization and experience of the team matched up against that focus, where do you feel the team is going to need the most help?
- Why do you win?
- Why do you lose?
- How do you feel about their ability to hit the mark in their messaging and positioning consistently?
- What's your opinion of the team's ability to open doors and effectively prospect?
- Is there a methodology or philosophy the team uses to execute?
- Do you feel the team is able to establish and hold close to the optimal pricing?
- How about their qualification skills?
- Presenting?
- Forecasting?
- Handoffs to delivery and client success?

Now, you'd probably like to know about the forecast . . . for both the team, but also the future of the company, right?

- What are the expectations over the next year? Five years?
- How is the team currently performing against expectations?
- Deal sizes? Win rates? Cycle lengths? What percentage of pipeline comes inbound versus the expectation of pipeline development from sales outbound efforts?

And finally, you'll want to ask questions about the fun element of the role. Think about the concepts of intrinsic inspiration to help understand not only the mindset of the team, but whether this will be a place where you will want to stay, grow, and advocate.

- In what ways do you recognize the performance of the team and celebrate it?
- How does what we sell impact our customers? How about their customers?
- What happens when a rep loses a big deal? How does the organization react?

- What investments do you make in the team beyond their compensation and benefits? What is the philosophy of the organization with regards to making those types of investments?
- How does the organization hold itself accountable to its own values and/or mission statement?

I could go on and on with questions aligned to the framework, but by now I am guessing you get the point. Bookmark these pages for your next interview or due diligence exercise.

YOU, THE INTERVIEWER

You have several sales candidates to interview. You are already using some of the questions I outlined earlier to assess the alignment. But how about the concepts of transparency and expectation setting?

You can use the structure of the Five F's to consider the questions you'd like to understand about the candidate. Where have they focused in their past roles, and what is their expertise? What roles have they played in the field, what territories, how large of a sales organization, what types of tools are they familiar with, and what resources do they feel they need and/or are reliant on? Talk about their fundamentals—strengths and weaknesses. Talk about past performance relating to their forecast, and finally dig into their culture fit through fun.

You won't miss a thing with the Five F's in your back pocket.

REP-BY-REP APPLICATION THROUGH INTRINSIC INSPIRATION

There will always be activities and behaviors your team members need to focus on that they just don't or won't want to. Maybe it's prospecting. Maybe it's their adherence to keeping their CRM up to date. It could be anything.

You have choices in how to handle it. Choice one? To be an autocratic overlord and attempt to create inspiration through threats. "You've got to hit your prospecting activity target five days in a row, or you're fired." Okay, maybe that's a touch extreme, but we tend to fall into inherent parental approaches as a leader. "Cut the lawn or no phone." Or choice two? Thinking about the fun part of the framework, using it to maximize the individual's intrinsic inspiration.

Can we take lessons from parenting and apply it to these moments? I see it in action every day.

My wife is a firm believer in the power of teaching children music, and there's plenty of science to back it up.[50] An article from Bright Horizons summed up our feelings on the subject perfectly:

> Music ignites all areas of child development and skills for school readiness, including intellectual, social-emotional, motor, language, and overall literacy. It helps the body and the mind work together. Exposing children to music during early development helps them learn the sounds and meanings of words.[51]

Every day, my wife spends time with our nine- and eleven-year-old, one at a time, on the piano. A lesson every day, and the lessons don't stop in the summer. As you might imagine, a nine- and an eleven-year-old aren't always intrinsically inspired to play the piano each day. Some days include one of them leaving the room and not coming back, filled with anger and frustration. How would you deal with resistance to something they both don't necessarily always enjoy, but is optimizing their learning ability?

Would you yell at them daily? Threaten to take away their iPads if they don't cut it out? Tell them that "we will sit here all day until you complete today's lesson"? You could—and with inflating levels of threats and yelling, it might work. Could you pay them to do their piano lessons? I guess . . . but that's not ideal.

Or, could you think about the areas that drive intrinsic inspiration and think about ways to utilize those?

Starting with recognition, we are driven to see the impact of our efforts. While we have not perfected this element as parents, the beginning approaches are paying off. For each song my wife determines that they have mastered, the song is put up on a chart and celebrated. The chart stays up and is getting longer and longer. It's recognition and status in that, as my 17-year-old stepdaughter walks by and sees a new song on the list, she says, "Hey! Nice job on getting another song mastered. That's awesome!" The result—pride of accomplishment. Nothing tangible. Entirely free. Inspiration to keep accomplishing more of something they don't always want to do. Can you do this as a sales leader for your team members? Absolutely!

The kids also earn independence through their work. There's a certain feeling of micromanagement that comes with one-on-one learning. Even when it is your mother, you'd prefer to make mistakes on your own. Instead of each lesson being entirely watched over, a shift was made to allow the children to earn free practice time. If the lessons are each an hour, where parts of each hour were debates involving, "I don't wanna do sight reading today!" The arguments would go away because the kids knew that every minute wasted was cutting into their autonomous practice time. During those times, my wife would leave the room, and they would have time to make the mistakes on their own and work on achieving mastery. Can you provide opportunities for your team to make mistakes on their own, in a safe environment? Of course!

There are likely ways we could better leverage the other means of maximizing their inspiration. The point is, instead of swinging the stick of extrinsic motivation, can you use these elements to light an internal fire?

With your team, the traditional means of driving behavior is through extrinsic motivation. The positive means are primarily through variable compensation; dollars, commissions, bonuses. The negative means are primarily through measures; quota attainment, performance plans, the possibility of losing your job. Flip it.

THE MACRO APPLICATION OF INTRINSIC INSPIRATION

There was a time in my career when I should have considered myself lucky to have a sales job. The supply of individuals in such positions was equal-to-higher than the demand. Sales leaders knew it, and treated sellers as such.

During the summer of 2021, there were over 700,000 sales jobs available on ZipRecruiter's website alone,[52] which excluded retail sales, realtors, and car sales. At the time, as a sales leader looking across your sales team, you would consider yourself lucky that those individuals are showing up every day. Imagine having to fill multiple positions within your sales team. The supply of sellers who meet your specific criteria was practically nonexistent. Your competition for those individuals was massive. How will you find them, draw them to your organization, hire them, and keep them?

Number of sales jobs listed on ZipRecruiter*

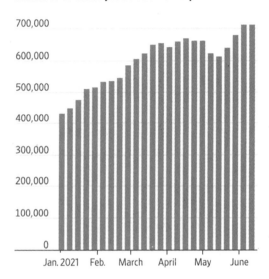

*Through June 14; Excludes real estate, cars, and retail sales
Source: ZipRecruiter

Find them. Interview them. Hire them. Keep them. All four are required. So, what is the traditional means of accomplishing this goal?

In the olden days, as discussed earlier in the book, leaders would: (a) Paint a picture of a five-star selling environment. "Our reps are making so much money, we're offering financial services consultants as a perk to help them better invest. One rep's back went out from having to stuff so much money into the wallet she was carrying around." That may bring the individual in, but it won't keep them when it's realized that perfection does not exist. Or (b) Paint a picture of a rapid career progression. "With our growth projections and hiring plans, you'll come in as an account executive, but the expectation is that you'll have opportunities to grow into management within the first year." Again, the overpromise-underdeliver is the fastest path to crushing intrinsic inspiration.

In a high-demand–low-supply environment, you could:

(a) Hire a bunch of recruiters: Either internally or externally, in an environment where there is overdemand and undersupply, this is likely an excellent investment. However, it's also the strategy of every other company of substance looking for that same talent.

(b) You could offer to pay the new sales hires more than anywhere else. However, this strategy is unsustainable, would require you to raise everyone's pay on the team, and do you want to compete on price? You wouldn't want your reps competing on price with prospects, so don't do it with your candidates and existing team members through their compensation, either.

Or, you could differentiate based on the environment you create. You could differentiate through the evidence that your sellers aren't turning over, they're excited to perform their best every day, and they are advocating on your behalf.

Regardless of when you're reading this, whether the supply/demand issue still exists, or has switched back to a more normal environment, wouldn't creating an environment where your sellers stay, do their best, and advocate be ideal? Hiring is expensive. Turnover is even more expensive. And what type of environment do you want to work in, yourself?

A focus on maximizing the environment for intrinsic inspiration wins! Looking across the six categories of intrinsic inspiration, let's think about the pandemic of 2020/2021 as a case study in driving inspiration.

LESSONS LEARNED FROM "THE GREAT RESIGNATION"

T HE U.S. BUREAU OF LABOR STATISTICS PUBLISHES DATA EACH MONTH on a statistic called *quits*. They describe this data point as "generally voluntary separations initiated by the employee," adding this rate "can serve as a measure of workers' willingness or ability to leave jobs."[53]

August of 2021 had a total of over 4.27 million people. This amount was the highest they had measured in a single month, since the bureau began measuring this data. This number surpassed the previous record from July, which surprised the previous record from April, which was just higher than June's. All 2021.

Whether you're reading during a continued high-turnover period or not, the remnants of the period serve as a considerable lesson for how to maximize performance, minimize turnover, and boost advocacy amongst your team.

Considering the elements that make up our intrinsic inspiration, the best leaders will use them naturally or keep them as a checklist. Am I helping the team with *predictability* through transparency, consistently considering *recognition* through feedback and praise, helping them recognize their *aim* means more than just their numbers, giving the team *independence* via trust and space to succeed, building *security* by showing the team I/we have their back, and treating them *equitably*?

When the pandemic hit . . .

In March of 2020, every business scurried to shelter like a pack of mice when the lights went on.

We all had to adjust.

At first, we shut off discretionary spend, sought ways to extend our runway by stockpiling the necessities (i.e., toilet paper), and looked to cut costs on those necessities as well. We learned how to optimally use technology. We could all handle a video call before, but it had to become the means to productivity and effectiveness.

From a behavioral perspective, two stages occurred. The first stage lasted a month or two, and the second stage lasted far too long. There is a third stage required, not only if you are reading this in 2022, but to create a unique adhesive to your company, the role, and to the individual team member's lasting performance.

STAGE 1: THE STRUGGLE BETWEEN SALES LEADERSHIP'S HUMAN DRIVE FOR PREDICTABILITY AND INDEPENDENCE

Like a basketball coach working with their team out on the court, sales leaders who were used to always seeing their teams during the day in the office suddenly had to adjust to their teams being out of sight. They lost their own ability to predict—through a lack of certainty. What are my team members doing? At first, those leaders were doing daily check-ins with their teams, everyone with their video on. They required a strict adherence to reporting and metrics, and the daily end-of-day check-ins consisted of a summary of their work for the day.

The leader drives the ship, which is why these calls became so pervasive. However, the good leaders recognized another human need: independence. We, as human beings, crave predictability—to have certainty. We crave control and autonomy. We thrive when we're trusted and provided the resources to do our jobs.

A balance was achieved. Self-aware leaders settled into a new balance between their own need to *predict* and their team members' need to have *independence*.

Suddenly, the next trend was upon us—a recognition that bonding would not form without a concerted effort and focus on it. We do our best when we feel safe, when we feel like others have our back, when we feel *security*. With everyone working remotely, there were individual pieces, but an eroding feeling of connection.

STAGE 2: THE OVER INDEX ON SECURITY

As we discussed in Chapter 12, we do our best in packs. Our brains are optimized when we are part of a family, where we have each other's backs and feel secure. But suddenly, our teams were all at home. While we spoke on the phone, over video, and connected via text and Slack, we were alone at work. Instead of check-ins focused on getting the leader what they needed, video calls were scheduled just to hang out. Zoom happy hours. Meet each other's children randomly making appearances during meetings, or their cat. Marketing departments sending piles of logoed swag home to every employee. It worked . . . for a few months.

However, the data points above, the rapid and record-breaking voluntary turnover, happened 10 months after this Stage 2 shift and continued for months. Why? Because sales leaders got stuck in Stage 2. There is nothing unique about this Stage 2 approach. Virtual happy hours and Zoom hang-outs can never replace the feeling of *security* established by being together, in the trenches with one another. Virtual can never replace the actual happy hours, the random meetings in the office kitchen, hallways, and parties and other establishments on the weekends.

RESIGNATION AND CHANGING JOBS BECAME EASY

From the time we moved into our home in 2009 to 2018, my house was an end-to-end Comcast Cable TV customer. We had cables running in from the ground, through the walls, into set-top boxes on four different TVs.

Every year, the price went up—but we dealt with it. There was a high *physical cost* to choosing an alternative—as that alternative was a satellite dish, which would require an installation from the roof, different devices with the TVs, and a similar pricing model. There was also a high *emotional cost* to choosing an alternative, as those set-top boxes had DVRs (digital video recorders), filled with my kid's favorite shows. There was no way to transfer the recordings. Get rid of the boxes, my kid's favorite episodes would go with them.

So, every year, we ate the higher cost because we felt the physical and emotional cost to change was too high.

That changed in 2018 with a recognition that we could remove the physical cost to change by just adding ROKU devices to the TVs, ditch the boxes and wires, and simply stream everything. We also realized that we could subscribe to my kid's favorite channels, and instead of just having their favorite episodes, we could do even better. We could now get *all* the episodes on demand whenever we wanted them.

We ditched the boxes, saved money, and added flexibility to watch from wherever we wanted. We signed up with AT&T NOW and kept them for two and a half years. During that period, the price never changed. And we happily paid it without even paying attention.

In March of 2021, AT&T NOW emailed us with the following message: "Due to increased programming costs, the price of your AT&T TV NOW package will increase to $94.99 a month, and your total monthly charge will go up by $9.99 starting with your 04/07/2021 payment."

It was the first price increase since we signed up. Within 10 minutes, I had canceled with AT&T and signed up on Fubo. Aside from a couple of channel differences, and at a benefit of a slightly lower investment than AT&T pre-price increase, there was very little disruption. Easy-peasy . . . same solution for less money, and a lot less money than the oncoming price increase.

The selling environment during the Great Resignation looked an awful lot like this story, didn't it? Changing sales jobs became like changing streaming TV service providers for your team members.

- The *physical cost* of changing jobs is practically nonexistent. Commute doesn't change . . . I still get out of bed, expend a few steps to the kitchen, then a few steps more into their home office. The salesperson receives a new laptop, maybe that pair of logoed socks in the mail, and off they go.
- The *emotional cost* of changing jobs is practically nonexistent. It's a whole lot easier to leave someone you've only met over the phone and video than your true friends and family, who you've spent hours with in the trenches, experiencing highs and lows together. If your salespeople are nearly entirely remote, they will have little emotional costs to leave.

In a largely remote environment, it is unlikely to take much to drive an individual who's working in your organization, whom you've never met, to suddenly take off. Simple things salespeople in the office have always been used to, just like a cable-TV price increase:

- "Quotas are going up!"
- "Your territory is going to be smaller this year."
- "You're getting a new manager (whom you've never met)."
- You're in a personal slump, having just lost an opportunity you were working on.
- Your friend tells you about how great the job and money is at her job . . . oh, and they're hiring!

Just like changing your streaming TV provider, the physical and emotional cost of a sales job change is lower than ever. There's not much you can do about the physical cost to change. But there is something unique to your organization you can do about the emotional cost.

STAGE 3: THE MISSING PIECE—*AIM* . . . OR "DOES MY WORK MATTER?"

Go beyond the forecast in your rep one-on-ones.

If your one-on-ones are all about the numbers and the forecast, you're doing it wrong. Spend some time understanding the true meaning of what your team is responsible for.

Do your reps know what their work means to you . . . on a personal level? What does their success mean to you and your life? Do you know what it means to your team members when they are successful? Have the conversation.

Do your reps know what their work means to the company? Can your salespeople see their impact? If not, help them to see it. This was one of the reasons why I loved working in and on smaller companies; I could see the impact beyond just my number.

Do your reps know what their work means to your customers? When your sales-people successfully close an opportunity, do they just move on? Or are they able to see how that customer is now more successful because of their efforts? Are they able to understand what that customer, who took a risk to buy from your rep and your company, can now do personally and professionally as a result?

Do your reps know what their work means to your customers' customer? When a customer of yours sells a product or service successfully, what does that mean to their customers? How are their lives better for it? Find out. Ask your customers.

If you're helping a company manufacture medical devices more efficiently and effec-tively, the result of your sale likely means you're saving lives.

At PowerReviews, we helped retailers and brands collect and display ratings and reviews on their websites. So what? We helped their end consumers make better decisions on where to spend their hard-earned money, creating better lives for those consumers. Cheesy? Maybe. But unique to our company and our competi-tors. Our team cared about ratings and reviews, not because it filled their own wallets, but because they cared about the impact their selling efforts had beyond just their number.

Your products and services' aim, mission, purpose, and impact are unique to your company. Figure out what it is. Embrace it. Make sure your team members know it and understand it. They won't all care, but the ones that do will likely stick around more, outperform the others, and help rally their network of like-minded individuals to want to join you.

You'll still have to raise quotas. You'll still have to reduce territory sizes. Reps will still lose deals, get new managers, and have friends who appear to be having the times of their lives. Reps will still leave. However, by embracing transparency around everything you do—and the *why* regarding the things you control—you will more often be the recipient of those job changers instead of the victim.

Go put it all to work.

> *There's something you can achieve without effort; failure.*
> *Nothing else.*
>
> — B. C. Forbes, *How To Get The Most Out of Business*, 1927

ADDITIONAL RESOURCES

SHAMELESS SELF-PROMOTION AND AN ASK

Congratulations! You finished the book—except for the acknowledgments that follow, which I hope are at least entertaining.

Three things to leave you with before you go . . .

ADDITIONAL RESOURCES

I share free stuff on just about every channel (my website, LinkedIn, Twitter, YouTube, Facebook, etc.), but the best place to start is probably my website, www.toddcaponi. com. As a side note, if you loved the quotes from sales' past that started each chapter, I share similar quotes week-daily at @SalesHistorian on both Twitter and Instagram, too. Or, check out *The Sales History Podcast* for deep dives into sales history topics.

AN ASK

If you've read all the way to here, could I ask you to do me just one favor? I'd love your feedback, in the form of a review wherever you picked up the book. Your *honest* reviews. If you thought it was a five, give it a five. If you thought it sucked, rate it as you will, and either way, let your peers know why in the form of a review.

Also, if you've been through one my workshops or keynotes, a review at G2.com under Sales Melon LLC would be much appreciated, too. The proliferation of feedback and everything we interact with is growing, and for good reason! Your opinion matters more than mine to others when it comes to the value of what I do.

SHAMELESS SELF-PROMOTION

Speaking of workshops or keynotes, those are what I do when I'm not writing. If you head over to www.toddcaponi.com, you'll find more information. But to save you the trip, the programs are designed to be one-part engaging and entertaining, two-parts head-slapping insights, and two-parts immediately actionable. Learn it. Use it. See the results.

For your revenue teams, the programs bring behavioral insights into how we as human beings engage, prioritize, decide, and ultimately buy. We then apply those learnings to your messaging, positioning, presenting, and negotiations. For your revenue leadership teams, the programs teach and reinforce much of what you just read in this book.

ACKNOWLEDGMENTS

WHEN I WROTE MY FIRST AND ONLY OTHER BOOK, *THE TRANSPARENCY Sale,* I was giving up a role as chief revenue officer of a company that was recognized as the fastest-growing in Chicago from 2014 to 2017. It was a huge leap. Given I also felt that the book would suck, because: (a) I had never written a book before, (b) I wasn't a writer, and (c) I had no idea what I was getting myself into. The odds that I would be back in a sales leadership role soon after the book had launched seemed high.

And now, a second book. I still can't believe the first one did so well and continues to grow as a standard in sales organizations. The first book won three awards. That's insane. And, my speaking and workshop business, Sales Melon LLC, is now in its fourth year and is thriving. Yes . . . that's a paragraph of shameless self-promotion.

I digress. Writing a second book is considerably different than writing a first. The process is surprisingly different. The time investment has also been considerably different, as I couldn't just take six months off the write this time . . . I'm running a business.

Lastly, the support needed was also different. For the first book, I needed encouragement that I was doing the right thing. I needed the confidence to know that what I was writing about mattered. Oh, and did I mention, I knew nothing about the publishing industry, didn't know how to structure a book much less write it, how to launch and promote, and how to build a business around it.

So, with this book, the thank-yous are of a different sort. They're the individuals who have helped the business thrive, because without that, I wouldn't have written this one. They're also the individuals who have taught me, challenged me, and provided insights that are reflected in these pages.

To start, my mentor Scott Anschuetz has been more helpful than he'll ever know. Without fail, we connect for a half hour every month for probably three years now. I leave those calls with two pages of notes coupled with the confidence and the drive to do something about them.

Two others that have made a bigger impact on my business more than they know: the co-founders of Chicago's Sales Assembly, Jeff Rosset and Matt Green. If you're in the tech space, look them up, and look up Sales Assembly as a resource for your teams. They made a big impact on my success at PowerReviews, but as I've launched and built my company and brand, they've been incredible supporters, referrers, and provided me with a platform to share my nonsense. They've become great friends, too. Thank you!

And how can I not thank Shawn Herring. As I wrote my first book, I honestly thought I'd write it, talk about it for a few months, and get a job again. I incorporated—making up what I thought was a funny company name (Sales Melon LLC) based on a line from the movie *So I Married an Axe Murderer*. I built a crappy website. Off I went. A few months in, I met up with Shawn in San Francisco. While I was still unsure of where my career would go, Shawn said something to me that stuck. "Todd, you have what every company wants: product-market-fit." That single comment refocused me, my confidence, and my business. Here we are . . . the business is exploding, I'm having a fantastic time, I'm publishing this book, and my investment in Advil is at an all-time low.

As you build your own business, you need a support system of not only likeminded individuals, but also those who will challenge you. The first person who has become a part of my virtual board is Jeff Bajorek. We quite literally have created pseudo board meetings around each other's businesses, which was such a helpful exercise and continues to be an amazing sounding board.

While there are others, I also wanted to give props to Lisa Murphy, who joined my company, Sales Melon, in the summer of 2021, and has served in an operational capacity to help me free up time to write this book and enhance every interaction I have with all of you.

Then there are the brilliant minds who you always want to stop, listen to, and learn from, like Amy Volas, Christina Brady, and Jordana Zeldin. If you're not following them, start.

A special thank you to some of the clients who have taught me, allowed me to experiment, helped me develop my programs more broadly, and in some cases caused ah-ha moments that made it into this book. Individuals like Ronny Sage (Founder and CEO of ShoppingGives), Robby Halford, Bryan Naas, Chris Patton, Larkin Kay, Ethan Zoubek, Josh Bean, and one non-client, who was a fountain of applications for transparency in leadership, Joey Nalevka.

And speaking of applications and learning from the best, let's start with my friend Kira Meinzer. If you don't have a good CHRO to work with at some point in your leadership career, you need it. Kira was that person for me. When we began working together, I had quite a bit of sales leadership experience. However, I didn't know what I didn't know about hiring, firing, planning, budgeting. She taught me so much.

Of course, none of this book is written without the great managers and leaders I've worked for in my career. Sue Hatton, whom I haven't talked to in years, was the first technology sales leader I worked for at Computer Associates, setting the bar for what *great* was in my eyes. CA was a challenging place to work, but it had some great sales leaders including Christopher O'Malley and Debbie Rosen.

After leaving Computer Associates, I went to SAP to work for Ed Lange. I learned so much from Ed about how to build a culture of accountability and teamwork and had so much fun I couldn't wait to get to work every day. Talk about a place full of incredible leaders, and an incubator for today's best. Watching my friend, who originally brought me to SAP in the 1990s, DJ Paoni, now President of SAP North America, do it absolutely the right way is amazing.

Later and for other companies I worked for individuals at early-stage tech companies like Steve Potts, Tom Meredith, Bruce Costello, Michael Lynch, and Steve Davis. There are so many who influenced my approach, made me better at what I do, and overall made work, and therefore life, so much more fulfilling.

Speaking of ExactTarget, their entire approach and sales leadership team was a case study in how culture and transparency done right pays off. Andy Kofoid may be the best ever, battling with Joe Kuntz for the crown. After running sales teams for early-stage tech companies, Andy saw something in me. I turned him down, writing an email with the three reasons why I couldn't come to ExactTarget at the time. He apparently saw a potential to excel in the big-time world of unicorn tech and helped me see the light. I'm so glad he did. Over my almost four years at Exact-Target, he trusted in me to own and grow a large divisional team, then to rebuild sales enablement from the ground up to support 20-plus new sales hires per month plus the 300 plus we already had around the globe, and so much more during and after. However, I would need an entire page to list out the awesomeness of that crew.

And, of course, Matt Moog, who hired me after interviewing 12 other candidates . . . many of whom were more experienced, and whom I knew and looked up to. He allowed me to build, challenge, experiment, and grow.

A special thank you to the master of the Non-Obvious, my publisher Rohit Bhargava and his team at Ideapress. I couldn't have written the first book without your expertise, guidance, and ideation. A constant focus on improvement made choosing to go with you again on this second book a no-brainer.

Thank you to my parents, as I wish my dad was still around to see this book. One of my favorite moments was sharing one of the first printed copies of my first book with him at the nursing home. He taught me more about sales and sales leadership than anyone on Earth. Growing up in a home where Dad went to work every day running sales teams, his personality and approach is what made me. He published a newsletter to his team, and in every issue there was a section called, "Todd Alan Says . . . " (yes, Alan is my middle name). It was a motivational tip, joke, or some other element made to brighten the day of the team. I was just a baby . . . so I wasn't saying anything at the time.

Last, the most important thank-you of them all go to my wife Christy, my kids Eden and Luke, and my stepdaughter Skye. You are why I do anything. I tell you face-to-face what you mean to me, so I'll leave the cheese to those interactions, but just so it's in writing: I love you and thank you!

The goal for you? If someone who works for you writes a book thanking those who made an impact on their career and their lives, be on that list. Whether leading an individual for weeks, months, or years, making the impact on others that these individuals above have made on me was always my goal. And years later, those standouts are never forgotten.

ENDNOTES

1. *Harvard Business Review*. 2021. "Our Brains Were Not Built for This Much Uncertainty."[online] Available at: <https://hbr.org/2021/09/our-brains-were-not-built-for-this-much-uncertainty>

2. Powerreviews.com. 2016. [online] Available at: <https://www.powerreviews.com/wp-content/uploads/2016/04/PowerofReviews_2016.pdf>

3. Team, P. 2021. "Survey: The Ever-Growing Power of Reviews - PowerReviews." [online] PowerReviews. Available at: <https://www.powerreviews.com/insights/power-of-reviews-survey-2021/>

4. Ibid.

5. DENT Neurologic Institute. 2021. "22 Facts About the Brain | World Brain Day." [online] Available at: <https://www.dentinstitute.com/posts/lifestyle-tips/22-facts-about-the-brain-world-brain-day/>

6. Bloomberg.com. 2009. "Are you a robot?" [online] Available at: <https://www.bloomberg.com/news/articles/2009-10-15/amazon-turning-consumer-opinions-into-gold>

7. Lipman, Victor. 2014. "Study: Management Transparency Motivates Employees," *Psychology Today*. [online] Available at: <https://www.psychologytoday.com/us/blog/mind-the-manager/201401/study-management-transparency-motivates-employees>

8. Einola, Katja, and Mats Alvesson. "The perils of authentic leadership theory." *Leadership* 17.4 (2021): 483-490.

9. Livescience.com. 2021. "Humans Smell Fear, and It's Contagious." [online] Available at: <https://www.livescience.com/24578-humans-smell-fear.html>

10. Lexico.com. 2022. "Confidence," def. N. 1.2. [online] Available at: <https://www.lexico.com/en/definition/confidence>

11. Lexico.com. 2022. "Confidence," def. N. 1. [online] Available at: <https://www.lexico.com/en/definition/confidence>

12. ATR Brain Information Communication Research Laboratry Group. 2016. "Manipulating brain activity to boost confidence: New breakthrough in neuroscience: Self confidence can be directly amplified in the brain." [online] Available at: <www.sciencedaily.com/releases/2016/12/161215085902.htm>

13. Cuddy, Amy. 2012. "Your Body Language May Shape Who You Are," TED Global. [online] Available at: <https://www.ted.com/talks/amy_cuddy_your_body_language_may_shape_who_you_are?language=en>

14. *Neuroscience News*. 2017. "'Power Poses' Don't Work, Studies Suggest." [online] Available at: <https://neurosciencenews.com/power-poses-psychology-7458/>

15. Statista. 2021. "Walmart annual revenue 2012-2019." [online] Available at: <https://www.statista.com/statistics/555334/total-revenue-of-walmart-worldwide/>

16. Sun, L. 2021. "Where Will Salesforce Be in 5 Years?" The Motley Fool. [online] Available at: <https://www.fool.com/investing/2021/01/12/where-will-salesforce-be-in-5-years/>

17. Bragger, J., Kutcher, E., Schettino, G., Muzyczyn, B., Farago, P., & Fritzky, E. (2016). "The Job Interview and Cognitive Performance: Does Structure Reduce Performance on Selection Batteries, and Can Explanation of Purpose Improve It?" *Performance Improvement Quarterly*, 29(2), 97-124.

18. Gallup News. 2015. "Managers Account for 70% of Variance in Employee Engagement." [online] Available at: <https://news.gallup.com/businessjournal/182792/managers-account-variance-employee-engagement.aspx>

19. "Wilson To Address First Sales Congress." *Los Angeles Herald*, 8 July 1916.

20. Black Enterprise. 2021. "7 Facts You Should Know about Shirley Ann Jackson." [online] Available at: <https://www.blackenterprise.com/seven-facts-shirley-jackson/>

21. Federal Trade Commission. 2021. "The Do Not Call Registry." [online] Available at: <https://www.ftc.gov/news-events/media-resources/do-not-call-registry>

22. Federal Trade Commission. 2021. "CAN-SPAM Act: A Compliance Guide for Business." [online] Available at: <https://www.ftc.gov/tips-advice/business-center/guidance/can-spam-act-compliance-guide-business>

23. Goodreads. 2022. "Erin Hunter Quotes." [online] Available at: <https://www.goodreads.com/author/quotes/27498.Erin_Hunter>

24. TheFreeDictionary.com. n.d. "Orchestrate," def. N. 2. [online] Available at: <https://www.thefreedictionary.com/orchestrate>

25. Sheldon, A. 1911. *The Art of Selling*. Libertyville, Illinois: The Sheldon University Press, p.18.

26. Adamson, B., Dixon, M., Toman, N., and Spenner, P. 2015. *The Challenger Customer*. New York, NY: Portfolio/Penguin, pp.35-56.

27. Abella, A. 2016. "Confused by Sales? A Basic Sales Funnel Explained." Due.com blog.

28. Tait, V. & Miller, J.H. 2019. "Loss Aversion as a Potential Factor in the Sunk-Cost Fallacy," *International Journal of Psychological Research*, 12(2), 8-16.

29. Kahn W.A. 1990. "Psychological conditions of personal engagement and disengagement at work," *The Academy of Management Journal*, Vol. 33 No. 4, pp. 692-724.

30. Centers for Disease Control. n.d. "Chronic Diseases in America" [online] Available at: <https://www.cdc.gov/chronicdisease/resources/infographic/chronic-diseases.htm>

31. Wisenberg Brin, D. 2021. "Why Don't Patients Follow Their Doctors' Advice?" AAMC [online]. Available at: <https://www.aamc.org/news-insights/why-don-t-patients-follow-their-doctors-advice>

32. Hendershot, K. 2017. "Doctor's Advice Most Often Ignored By Patients." Covenant Health [online] Available at: <https://www.covenanthealth.org/healthcalling/2017/august/doctors-advice-most-often-ignored-by-patients/>

33. Damasio, A. 2005. *Descartes' Error*. New York: Penguin Books.

34. Péronnet F, Mignault D, du Souich P, Vergne S, Le Bellego L, Jimenez L, Rabasa-Lhoret R. "Pharmacokinetic analysis of absorption, distribution and disappearance of ingested water labeled with D_2O in humans." *European Journal of Applied Physiology*. 2012 Jun;112(6):2213-22. doi: 10.1007/s00421-011-2194-7. Epub 2011 Oct 14. PMID: 21997675; PMCID: PMC3351614.

35. Failory.com. 2021. "Startup Failure Rate: Ultimate Report + Infographic." [online] Available at: <https://www.failory.com/blog/startup-failure-rate>

36. Gage, D. 2021. "The Venture Capital Secret: 3 Out of 4 Start-Ups Fail," *Wall Street Journal*. [online] Available at: <https://www.wsj.com/articles/SB10000872396390443720204578004980476429190>

37. Gallup News. 2019. "More Harm Than Good: The Truth About Performance Reviews."[online] Available at: <https://www.gallup.com/workplace/249332/harm-good-truth-performance-reviews.aspx>

38. Ariely, D. 2016. *Payoff*. Simon & Schuster, pp. 18-21.

39. Stockton, N. 2014. "What's Up With That: Your Best Thinking Seems to Happen in the Shower," *Wired*. Available at: <https://www.wired.com/2014/08/shower-thoughts/>

40. Zadow AJ, Dollard MF, Dormann C, et al. 2021. "Predicting new major depression symptoms from long working hours, psychosocial safety climate and work engagement: a population-based cohort study," BMJ Open;11:e044133. doi: 10.1136/bmjopen-2020-044133

41. Richardwiseman.com. 2021. [online] Available at: <http://richardwiseman.com/resources/The_Luck_Factor.pdf>

42. Missner, Marshall. 1985. "Why Einstein Became Famous in America." *Social Studies of Science* 15, no. 2 (1985): 267–91. http://www.jstor.org/stable/285389.

43. Brody, J. 2017. "The Surprising Effects of Loneliness on Health," *New York Times*. [online] Available at: <https://www.nytimes.com/2017/12/11/well/mind/how-loneliness-affects-our-health.html>

44. Wikipedia. 2021. "Survivor (American TV series)." Wikipedia. [online] Available at: <https://en.wikipedia.org/wiki/Survivor_(American_TV_series)>

45. Gallup News. 2021. "Why We Need Best Friends at Work." [online] Available at: <https://www.gallup.com/workplace/236213/why-need-best-friends-work.aspx.>

46. Yeginsu, C. 2018. "U.K. Appoints a Minister for Loneliness," *New York Times*. [online] Available at: <https://www.nytimes.com/2018/01/17/world/europe/uk-britain-loneliness.html.>

47. NeuroLeadership Institute. 2021. "Make the Most of Virtual Meetings by Learning to Reduce Your 'Distance Bias.'" [online] Available at: <https://neuroleadership.com/your-brain-at-work/virtual-meetings-reduce-distance-bias/>

48. Vassar, G. 2014. "Does your brain state make you smarter?" Lakeside. [online] Available at: <https://lakesidelink.com/blog/lakeside/does-your-brain-state-make-you-smarter/>

49. History.com 2019. "Great Recession." [online] Available at: <https://www.history.com/topics/21st-century/recession>

50. Møller, C., et al. 2021. "Audiovisual structural connectivity in musicians and non-musicians: a cortical thickness and diffusion tensor imaging study." Scientific Reports 11.1 (2021).

51. Brighthorizons.com. 2021. *Children and Music: Benefits of Music in Child Development*.

[online] Available at: <https://www.brighthorizons.com/family-resources/music-and-children-rhythm-meets-child-development>

52. Thomas, P. 2021. "The Pay Is High and Jobs Are Plentiful, but Few Want to Go into Sales," *Wall Street Journal*. [online] Available at: <https://www.wsj.com/articles/the-pay-is-high-and-jobs-are-plentiful-but-few-want-to-go-into-sales-11626255001>

53. U.S. Bureau of Labor Statistics. 2021. "Job Openings and Labor Turnover Summary." [online] Available at: <https://www.bls.gov/news.release/jolts.nr0.htm>

INDEX